YACHTSMAN'S
GPS
HANDBOOK

YACHTSMAN'S
GPS
HANDBOOK

A Guide to the Global Positioning System of Satellite Navigation

COLIN JONES

WATERLINE

Published by Waterline Books
an imprint of Airlife Publishing Ltd
101 Longden Rd, Shrewsbury, England

ISBN 1 85310 470 1

A Sheerstrake production.

A CIP catalogue record of this book
is available from the British Library

Typeset by Servis Filmsetting Ltd, Manchester

Printed in England by Livesey Ltd, Shrewsbury.

The compact GPS Mk 4 from Philips Navigation AS.

Contents

You can learn much about GPS and its operation just by studying the keyboard of the Philips GPS MkVI. (*Photo courtesy Philips Navigation AS*)

Chapter 1

The Biggest Step Forward

The very name Global Positioning System (GPS) is itself undoubtedly the most accurate description of the greatest position fixing and navigational step forward which man has taken since the ancient Chinese realised that lodestone has the peculiar property of always aligning itself North and South.

The revolution is global in two senses of the word. In the first place, a person standing anywhere in the world at any time of day or night will be able to receive information showing exactly where he is at that moment. In the second sense of the word, GPS is open to all members of all races as long as they are in possession of a mechanism capable of receiving and decoding the signals.

The proper name 'Navstar Global Positioning System' is even more descriptively accurate because it connotes 'a star to steer her by'. In this case we have twenty-one artificial stars called satellites travelling around the planet Earth, some 11,000 miles out, in precisely monitored orbits and constantly sending back a stream of information which can be used to calculate a position.

More of this later but — like all artificial position fixing devices — GPS relies on radio signals and makes the normal, artificial, navigational premise 'I know exactly where I am and I know at what speed my signals travel. I also know the time at which the signal was transmitted, so if you note its arrival time, we can soon work out how far you are from me'. This is a hi-tech version of the elementary school mathematics problem which poses, 'A train leaves station X at noon and moves at sixty miles per hour for three hours. How far will it have travelled by 1615?'

In practice, some confusion arises because there have been other systems and commercial organisations using variations of the duo-syllabic titles Navstar and Satnav, but the Global Positioning System has no connection whatsoever with these. Thus, to avoid any possible ambiguity, the first word of the full title is usually dropped and the remainder shortened to initials in the upper case, when we are talking about the present space miracle. We shall follow convention and cut our print bill by using the near acronym GPS throughout the book.

To those of us with a meagre scientific background, it might seem strange that we can derive a much more accurate indication of our position from satellites circling out in space than we can from a similar navigation method sitting on land less than a hundred miles away. In fact, the very high orbit is an essential ingredient of the success and certainly one important reason why GPS is much more precise than its predecessors — the most important of which have been Decca, Loran-C and Satnav. The altitude of the satellite orbit is important because it moves the signal transmitters away from all the polluting, weakening and warping effects of Earth and its occupants.

We should, however, also remember that GPS is primarily a military tool, so it needs to be reliable and accurate. If not, the attacker risks shooting down his own aircraft because he is not exactly sure where they are in relation to the enemy, or he could send his rockets hurtling into friendly forces because the positional data is inaccurate.

This very need for perfect precision necessitated finding a system which was impervious to jamming by the enemy and which would retain an accuracy of fifteen metres, or better, without being made less precise by night and day effects, seasonal changes, deteriorating weather and alterations in signal characteristics caused by their passage through different atmospheric conditions, or even as do radio waves when they cross a land/sea boundary.

All these natural and unnatural phenomena have created less than perfection and diminished reliability in the practical applications of most other position fixing systems.

The very rigorous parameters laid down by the military meant that only an organisation as large and powerful as the government of the United States of America could and would make the necessary investment in time and resources, not only for the research and development, but also to launch the space modules and to fine-tune where they needed to be placed in space. After much debate, the national funds were only made available to the US Department of Defense on condition that the end result — or at least a very large part of it — should be made available for wider, non-military use.

This is where the rest of us have scored lucky, but it also explains why some of the few problems occur to civilian users of the GPS system. Other countries of the world can receive and use the signals coming from the satellites, even though they have not contributed a single cent towards its invention, nor given any part of the billions of dollars it has cost to equip the birds and to get them to fly.

At the moment, civilian access to GPS is limited to only a part of the total transmitted signal and this is less precise than that employed by the military. There are now a number of simple, but clever, electronic ways to restore the potential fifteen metre accuracy, but these are not cheap and are not universally available because of a mixture of military pride, politics and greed.

This is to be regretted, because GPS is capable of almost limitless adaptation and utilisation. As soon as you comprehend the principle of numbered latitude lines and longitude lines crossing each other, every square metre of land or sea can be given a very precise address, made up from a combination of these North/South and East/West numbers — a grid, or the sort of matrix familiar to the users of even the most elementary maps.

This addressing device is obviously much used at sea where there are no landmarks against which a position can be referenced, or in relation to which a voyager can be given directions about when to turn, because he has reached a particular tree, a building or a crossroads. All such land locations generally have an address name, or a street name, a number, or a zip-code. In spite of its usual sea and aeronautical use, latitude and longitude could also be used to describe the location of terrestrial sites, in addition to one defined by a National Grid Reference system. Even these two could be easily trans-lated from one to another by a simple computer program.

The day is not too far off when a street map will have house numbers, names and a lat/long location identifier. If these were all stored on a computer database, the traveller would be able to dial up any of these addresses and be told by a combination of GPS and the digitised map how to get from his present position to the desired location.

One of the earliest applications of this exciting possibility was pioneered by a bus company wishing to avoid the inefficiency felt by a passenger who waits an hour for a bus, then three arrive within minutes of each other. Each vehicle's position is calculated by a GPS receiver and this data is shown on a screen at the company base. A radio voice link is then used to space out the buses.

Carried a step further into the haulage and carriage trades, deliveries would be made more on schedule and there would not be fuel wasted by drivers covering unproductive miles seeking elusive, little-known proper-ties. The advantages to emergency and rescue services, who are often frustrated by not knowing how to find a particular spot in a hurry, could be enormous. The problem area would be shown on a VDU screen, either in the mobile unit or at a controller's console, where the vehicle's position would also be flashing. The controller would be able to 'talk-in' the mobile on a screen map overlay, or even to send a different unit. Such a set-up could also monitor traffic congestion and pick a route to avoid it. The system has worked well to speed up sea rescue and to make seafaring safer. The land is sure to follow.

So will the air. GPS is a three dimensional system which is able to fix an aircraft's position in relation to flat space and to altitude. Its up-date method is fast enough even to record aircraft at supersonic speed, but is also sufficiently precise and versatile to tell a climber how far around a mountain he has moved and how high above sea level he has climbed. Simple computer arithmetic will then tell him both the altitude remaining and the distance to the summit.

If you can always know precisely where a unit is located and can monitor its speed, it is only a short step to issuing radio commands to move its direction controls and travel rate. You could then have total, robotic long distance control of just about any moving object.

We who dabble in electronics certainly live in exciting times. We also live in times which can be irritating for writers.

To avoid misunderstanding, the author wishes to announce from the outset that the terms 'he' and 'him' have been used to mean both male and female. There is nothing sexist nor neglectful about this. It is a writer's device to encourage the text to flow without constantly needing to reiterate 'he or she' and — even worse — him/her. Likewise the word 'man' has been used to signify both men and women, pilots and lady pilots, policemen and policewomen. In an office where at least fifty per cent of the work is done by one person of each sex and the GPS units on our boat are used by us both, no suggestion of bias would even make it past the typists and editors onto the page.

So we trust those of you who will read this book will have as much pleasure from it as we have enjoyed in its compilation.

Chapter 2

Introducing the Miracle

The Global Positioning System is much more than its name suggests because, in addition to telling you where you are, it is also a total navigation method. The on-board GPS unit (in car, boat, aircraft or on horseback etc) will inform you of your speed, your direction of travel, the direction you should take and when you will get to your destination. It can give this last piece of information in the number of minutes it will take to get there, or will convert this to an Estimated Time of Arrival in clock time.

GPS is a dynamic system, ie it constantly updates every item the navigator needs both in terms of geography (or position) and speed, or time — which are much the same thing in navigational terms.

In practical terms GPS is old/innovative technology able to do many new and exciting things at an incredible speed, but it still utilises very old navigational, algebraic and trigonometrical functions. That these functions are generated by computers and passed by microwaves means little to the practical navigator. He could find his way about the planet Earth without knowing much about the theory of the system. After all, you can drive a car, or use a computer, without looking at the mechanism. But, how much more confidently you use these machines when you understand a little of how they work.

The mechanical details of GPS and of the satellites follows.

The Satellites
Proper name: Navstar Global Positioning Service Satellite
Size: 5.2 metres (17ft) when solar panels are extended
Weight: 860kg (1,900lb) approx.
Altitude: 10,900 nautical miles
Orbital Arc: 55° to plane of equator
Orbit time: One circumnavigation every twelve hours
Life expectancy: Seven and a half years to replacement
Total constellation: Twenty-one operational satellites and three spares

Figure 1

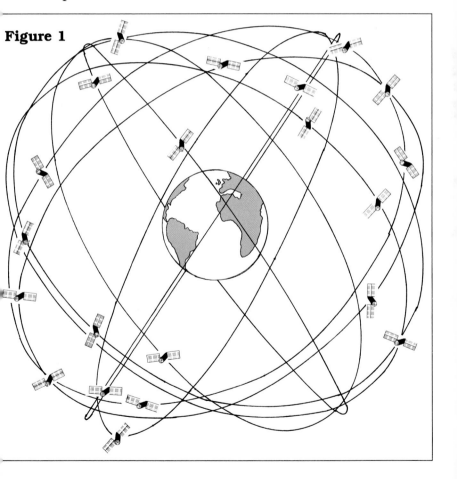

The present satellite armoury grew out of the experience which the engineers got with the old Block One orbiters, which were too low, too slow and not using the best parts of the radio frequency spectrum. In its day, it gave what then seemed like excellent assistance to the US Navy and to the cruising yachtsman able to afford military prices for the equipment. However, the surge in rocket technology and the regular delivery of payloads into outer space enabled the scientists to come up with something better.

The Block Two satellites are a design and engineering concept which is very far removed from that of their predecessors, but you will observe that there is nothing complex in understanding that there are twenty-one satellites orbiting regularly 10,900 nautical miles out in space in such a basketwork pattern that an antenna almost anywhere on our planet will be able to 'see' more than the three satellites needed to give a basic cocked hat position fix. These are not the so-called 'geo-stationary' satellites which are set to hover above a particular country, in order to give constant quality to the television signals which it is receiving from another part of the globe. The GPS space modules have been set in motion along tracks which do not follow the rotation of the Earth, but crisscross its axis in a pattern calculated to put the greatest number of usable satellites where they are most needed at appropriate times of the day. The dynamic mathematics involved in planning these orbits is a fantastic achievement in its own right.

You will observe that we are already using traditional navigational language and must assume that the reader is familiar with the parallels of latitude and the meridians of longitude and can find his way about the compass in order to practise position fixing, plotting and other pilotage skills and conventions. If you can navigate using parallel rules and dividers, together with a bit of arithmetic brain-power, then you will certainly perform the same tasks more easily by letting the GPS and the computers in the receiver do all the complex calculations for you.

Anybody who has ever used Decca or Loran-C, will very soon be at home with GPS instruments, whose conventions, displays and terminology have generally been taken from these land based systems.

The only confusion is likely to be in understanding how and what types of signals and messages the orbiters send and how they are interpreted by the receivers on land, at sea, or in the air to give a position, which might not be quite as accurate as many salesmen suggest, nor quite as phenomenally precise as some members of the press have eulogised us into believing. As we go along, you will come to recognise just how powerful GPS can be, but also see that steps sometimes have to be taken to eliminate potential errors deliberately induced into perfection by a combination of politics and economics.

Each visible satellite needs to tell the navigator two important pieces of data. Firstly where it is right now and secondly the time, annotated in a format which is very, very accurate and measurable in units small enough to cope with the huge relative velocity of a satellite moving one way and the Earth another. This means that vast distances are covered in fractions of a second, so the timekeeping hardware needs to be able to cope.

To get this basic information down to earth, the transmitter on board the satellite employs signals very like those used for radio and television, ie a mixture of electrical and magnetic energy blasted away from an antenna at so many pulses, or cycles per second. The number of positive to negative wave oscillations per second is called the frequency. As radio waves travel at the speed of light, Cycle (or pulse) Number 1 will have travelled a known distance before Cycle 2 is released. The distance between the high (positive) points of these two pulses is called the wavelength. Obviously the faster the pulses are released, the higher the frequency of emission and the shorter the wavelength. Put simplistically, a long wavelength, with longer distances between peaks takes longer for Peak 1 to get clear of the antenna before Peak 2 can be released.

17

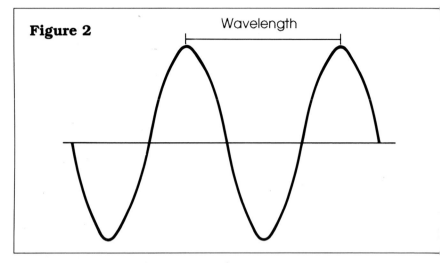

Figure 2

Wavelength

In the case of GPS, the frequency is very high (ie the pulsations are of short and rapid duration) creating an operating spectrum which is nearly at microwave-oven level. This has a number of very important radio propagation advantages, including a high resistance to all sorts of interference.

Out in space, this interference can be from sun spots and other solar radiation. Closer to Earth, there is the effect of the ionospheric layer, which can do some very startling things to radio reception. Down near the Earth's surface, there are literally millions of man-made radio-style and electronic signals running around in every direction imaginable. You can then add to these all the electrical noises made by heating thermostats, industrial welders, vehicle ignition systems and the sort of effect you get on your car radio when you pass underneath high tension cables. Finally, all mechanically propelled platforms have their own intrinsic noises created by everything from the car or boat ignition to spurious signals emitted by computers. There is so much radio magnetic 'mush' permanently all around us that it is a wonder that any signal ever reaches its intended destination in legible form.

In our dealing with a combination of time, speed and distance, if both the satellite and the signal's target destination were stationary, the measurement of — say — a boat's distance from the space capsule would be no more complicated than the sort of school maths problem which we have already touched on, but which could be redefined here as: ' If a car leaves A at 12.00hrs and travels at a constant 50mph, where will it be at 13.00?' Answer,' It will be somewhere on a circle at 50 miles range from A'. Notice that we know the distance, but there is no indication of the actual direction, which could be anywhere along a circle of radius 50 miles from the start point.

Figure 3

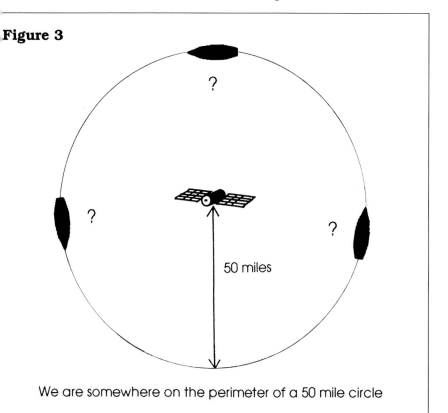

We are somewhere on the perimeter of a 50 mile circle

Space engineers always talk in nautical miles, which is a term and a distance recognisable by air pilots and sea navigators and we are at ease with its use. In broad terms, the nautical mile (at 6,080ft) is about 15.15 per cent longer than the statutory mile whose 5,280 feet length was decided by a whim of Her Majesty Queen Elizabeth The First. The engineers most often use the term 'satellite ranging' when they are discussing position fixing.

The microwave travels from orbit to Earth at about 163,000 nautical miles (nm) per second so, even if the satellite was right above you, it would still only need 6/100 (0.06) of a second to make the trip. Unfortunately, in that time the satellite would also have moved about 200 metres, so we already have a problem and a possible source of error. We have already moved away from the fundamental concept that we can only measure distance by radio signal very accurately if we are completely sure of the exact point of signal release. Near enough is not good enough with such a system.

The solution to this very complex dynamic problem is very neat. The engineers make the satellite and the receiver generate the same complex set of signal codes — call them digits, or varying size pulses — at exactly the same time. They are called Pseudo-Random codes, but they have nothing false nor random about them. The pulsations have deliberately been made so complicated that there is no danger of ambiguity, nor of mistaking one time segment for another. Even though we are dealing with very small fractions of a second, the technology is so good that the peaks and the troughs of the codes are generated to coincide totally in time and phase and height both at the sending end and at the Earth station.

This means that the receiver will be able to recognise the precise nanosecond that the pulse left the satellite's aerial.

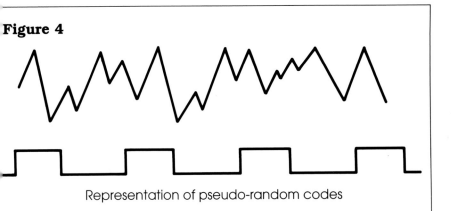

Figure 4

Representation of pseudo-random codes

Equally, because the space module is in a very precise orbit, travelling friction-free in a vacuum, its speed and direction are known in equally precise terms for every microsecond of every day. So, a number-crunching computer on a ship can quickly compute its own range (distance) from the satellite and this can be described as an arc on a chart, ie the computer knows that it is somewhere on the circumference of a precise distance circle whose centre is the satellite transmission aerial. Because timing is so important, engineers also frequently talk of range in terms of time rather than distance, ie the target is 1.847 seconds from the satellite.

It is obvious that this will only work if both the transmission clock and the receiving clock are very accurately synchronised and both are totally correct as UCT — Universal Co-ordinated Time. The pseudo-random codes work well, but can only give accurate distance data if both clocks are accurate to the nearest millionth of a second. So, the problem now shifts to synchronising the clocks.

The satellite clocks are super, super accurate. That they are called atomic clocks has nothing to do with nuclear energy but they are so named because they are controlled by a single atom of a substance which oscillates at a constant and known frequency of so many million times per second. If an atomic clock says that it is noon, it means precisely that — not a millionth of a second past twelve. This is why each one costs $1,000,000 — and there are four in each orbiter.

At the receiving end, we are closer to digital watch technology — which is good, but not atomic clock good — so our receiver timepiece could be a second fast, or perhaps half a second slow. If the satellite says that it sent a certain part of the code at 1200, but the boat clock made the time one thousandth of a second before noon, the difference would cause a distance discrepancy, or a position fix inaccuracy of about 163 nautical miles. More of this later.

The totally amazing GPS technology has another very clever piece of engineering working in favour of boats, land vehicles and aeroplanes, which obviously cannot carry the enormous dish antennae normally associated with satellite communication. In radio terms, transmission and reception efficiency is as much a function of the aerial as of the actual radio set and this generally means the bigger the better. This is seen in the huge dish antennae used by commercial stations and also in the dish aerials decorating houses indulging in satellite television. They compare very unfavourably with the small GPS aerials which I have on my boat.

Firstly, television satellites are (geo) stationary so can be accessed by a fixed directional antenna, whose capture effectiveness is increased by its saucer shape, which funnels all the energy into the central rod. Television signals carry a vast amount of information in order to create the moving images, the separate colours and the audio. This is a very power-hungry medium.

By contrast, the GPS antenna must be omni-directional, simultaneously to track several moving satellites over the total 360 degrees of the horizon and at varying degrees of altitude above it. Luckily, the amount of transmitted information is not enormous compared to — say — television, but because of the distances involved and the impossibility of installing very high powered, voltage gobbling transmitters aboard solar powered satellites, the signal strength is quite feeble when it reaches Earth.

There is an amplifier in the GPS antenna, but because this is not enough, the engineers very cleverly put an electronic nuisance to work. Again simplistically, their argument goes as follows.

All radio devices create their own internal background noise, which is almost exactly similar to the ultra, ultra rapid pulsations of electromagnetic energy and not too dissimilar from the GPS pseudo-random codes which we discussed earlier. You can hear this for yourself on any radio and even when a computer drive motor is leaking radio frequency energy into your radio or television. The fluctuations occur many millions of times per second and are so numerous and so rapid that they are indistinguishable to the human ear. They can, however, be traced by a computer-managed oscilloscope and the rises and falls can be ultra rapidly plotted.

With so much energy available at such rapidity, the statistical probability is that you can find a set of these oscillations whose peak and trough pattern closely resembles that of the GPS signal coming in, ie it will have highs and lows in about the same place.

By sliding the internal irritant signals about so that their highs and lows coincide with the same pattern in the GPS signal, double strength is created. If you like, the on-board coincident noise adds to the received signal of the same amplitude and makes it twice as loud. If you get good signal and noise, you have good GPS accuracy and many good GPS receivers have a display showing the signal to noise ratio and — hence — the quality and reliability of the positional data. (See Fig 5)

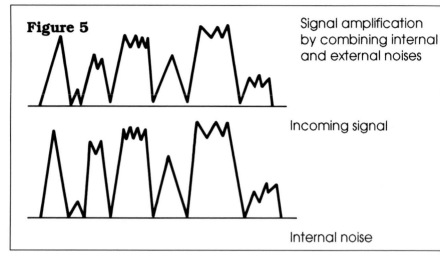

Figure 5

Signal amplification by combining internal and external noises

Incoming signal

Internal noise

Position fixing is not a new science and it has long been realised that if you know your distance from any two other points, you can establish where you are in relation to them. In theory, you could be at either of two places defined by where the distance radii from our two reference points cross. These are marked X on the illustration. In practice this problem usually solves itself because one of the theoretical position fixes is in a ridiculous place. (Fig 6)

Boat skippers regularly meet this phenomenon when they obtain a position 'B' estimating their distance off — say — a lighthouse and a beacon. If they did the reductio ad absurdum and actually drew the full arcs of their estimations, one of the intersect points would probably be well inland.

If we now add a third reference distance to our position fixing schema, we eliminate the ambiguity and a definite, precise location is proven. In the illustration (Fig 7) the actual distances from the fixed reference points 'A', 'B' and 'C' are 3 cm, 4 cm and 5 cm respectively. If they were lighthouses etc and we were using a different scale, there is only one place on Earth which is 300 metres from Lighthouse 'A', 400 metres from Buoy 'B' and 500 metres from Water Tower 'C'.

Figure 6

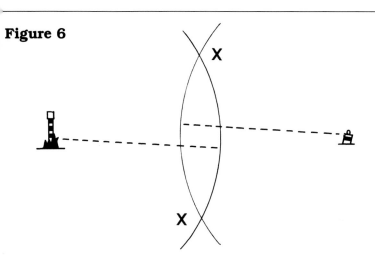

We could be at either of the places marked 'X'

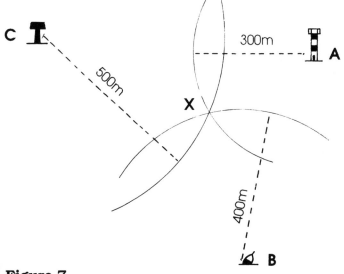

Figure 7

Three known distances gives a definite position at 'X'

In visual marine navigation, we would probably use compass bearings instead of distances and the derived position lines rarely cross at exactly one place, but are more likely to create the navigator's 'cocked hat', which says that the boat is somewhere inside a small triangle. However, those navigators who have used Decca, Loran-C or any of the more local radio position-fixing media, will be very familiar with the position-by-distance principles used by GPS. What they might not realise is that a cocked hat is very rare in navigation using this aid. It is capable of precision to within a few centimetres.

Just here, we discover a minor hiccup because we have not mentioned altitude. We know where we are, but we are not sure of our place on an altitude scale. Happily, in practical terms, this is a very minor irritant and there are many ways of removing it. The problem is only mentioned because it explains why mariners are required to enter the height of the antenna above sea level when setting up a newly-installed GPS unit. The aircraft pilot can pass this information to the navigation computer from his altimeter, or his system will establish altitude by reference to a fourth satellite.

To keep things pure and simple and to follow the democratic protocol that there are many more mariners than aviators using GPS, from here on we shall assume that all our required position fixes and routes are at sea level. That is to say that we shall ignore the third diameter (3D) and work in two dimensional only (2D) which is right and proper for sea crossing. The performance of GPS in 2D mode is quite phenomenal.

Let us now return to understanding satellite ranging and assume that our on-board GPS receiver has locked on to three satellites and has decoded the information that we are five seconds from satellite 'A', seven seconds from satellite 'B' and nine seconds from satellite 'C' at the precise time that these orbiters transmitted the signal segment that our GPS computers are currently processing.

We now have a very precise position fix .... but .... what if our on-board clock is a second slow? It would see distance 'A' as six seconds, 'B' as eight seconds and 'C' as ten seconds and would show us a position far removed from reality. The distance circles would intersect well away from where they should and the cocked hat would be enormous.

Notice that the position-fixing line derived from satellites 'A' and 'B' still intersect at X, but the intersects proposed by 'C' are nowhere near this point. The geometry is suggesting that our boat could be at any of the positions 'X', 'Y' or 'Z' or might be at any other place within the elliptical triangle (cocked hat) formed by them. (Fig 8)

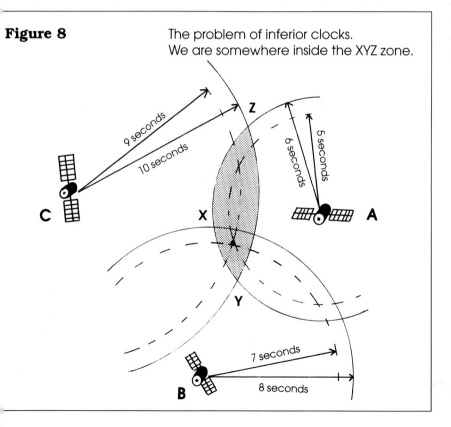

Figure 8

The problem of inferior clocks.
We are somewhere inside the XYZ zone.

9 seconds

10 seconds

Z

6 seconds

5 seconds

C

X

A

Y

7 seconds

8 seconds

B

Go back, for a moment, to radio waves theoretically travelling at the speed of light (186,000 statute mps) which means that our one second slow boat clock is showing an over-shoot distance of about 163,000 nautical miles. This is bad news and good news. The bad is a very serious posfix error and the good is that some of the positions postulated by our clock calculations are so ridiculous that they may even be well away from the Earth's surface, so can be ignored.

It is now time for the computers and their incredible number and data handling speed and capacity to take over. They have been programmed to observe that the three positional lines do not exactly intersect, so there must be something wrong. They then set off on a hunt to find a place where a directly proportional time/distance alteration to all three components would give an exact intersection. Put another way, they go on a controlled search by rapidly adding or subtracting microseconds to each parameter until an intersect point is found. (Fig 9)

Remember that there is only one practical place where this can happen and this removes the need for haphazard, random searches by the computers. They are also programmed for probability, which causes them to ignore the impossible and the very improbable and to search in the most likely direction for a coincident point which they can display with total certainty that it is where the clock in the receiver is located.

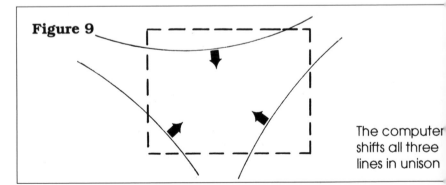

Figure 9

The computer shifts all three lines in unison

Once this very precise point is located, the computer then calculates that our on-board clock is one second slow and it will apply this correction to all subsequent received data. The speed at which these calculations are made seems incredible to the layman, but we are getting better about appreciating and understanding such science. You have but to look at the dial of your digital watch counting in hundredths of a second to realise that this sort of technology is now becoming very ordinary. The word processor on which this is being written takes only about five seconds to count a chapter's 4,000 words and to arrange them in alphabetical order ready to have their spelling checked. It is this sort of engineering which makes GPS possible.

In the real world, a GPS receiver clock running a whole second out of step would be extremely rare. The on-board chronometer of a good receiver gets its time as part of the signal received directly from those atomic clocks in the satellite. The distortion effects of the atmosphere and circuitry can create small anomalies but we are talking of amounts not discernible to even the fastest human eye. We have carried various GPS sets on the boat for over five years now and have never managed to spot a discrepancy between the GPS clock and any other time source available. Clock time problems are not something the GPS owner needs to worry about.

All these marvellous mathematical and position display computations have assumed that the satellite is stationary. Because this is not the case, the computers need to apply another set of corrections to compensate for the satellite's change of position (or time/distance change) between when the data segment was sent and when it was received. Fortunately there are several factors which make this a relatively straightforward mathematical task.

Firstly, the satellites have been very precisely placed into orbital paths and once set in motion they go on circling the Earth in a friction-free vacuum. In theory there is nothing to slow them down, nor to speed them up.

They are also continuously monitored by the Earth
tracking stations, whose own very sophisticated equipment can tell if the top of the satellite antenna has been
rotated a couple of degrees, or pulled a couple of centimetres off track by the gravitational effects of Earth and
of other planets.

The engineers can either correct this if it is serious,
but more often send a correction up to the satellite
which re-transmits it to the GPS receiver unit which
then corrects its own data. We are not here talking about
a major program re-write, but about altering two words
in one sentence of a whole chapter. This so-called
ephemeris information is stored in an almanac aboard
the satellite, which constantly transmits information
about itself and is also contained in a similar almanac in
the best GPS receivers. These extra facilities and the
extra receiver computers needed to process the data
partly explains why there is a vast price difference
between poor and excellent GPS equipment and why the
latter are faster, steadier and more accurate. They simply
have more going for them to increase rate and precision.

Chapter 3

Is It Worth It?

Even though GPS has now been functional for several years, there are still a number of questions hanging over its acceptance by the world-wide users. These queries are not about its theoretical and proven practical performance, but are more tied up with its comparison with other position-fixing systems, with economics, with politics and with where the individual lives and works.

In any comparative debate over the merits and demerits of space orientated GPS as opposed to such land based radio navigational systems as Decca and Loran-C, it has to be admitted that both sides have good points and bad: strengths and weaknesses.

The terrestrial systems are proven technology with transmitters sited so that they are easily accessible for repair and periodic maintenance. There are many thousands of Decca and Loran-C receivers in use and there is a good coverage of equipment suppliers and service agents. Both systems are likely to be kept alive for many years.

Unfortunately, land generated radio signals also suffer some disadvantages. Their use as a position fixer normally requires a Master Station and up to three Slave transmitters. Signals from all four arrive at the receiver, which calculates its position from the phase difference between them. Put very simply, the frequency/speed of radio wave travel is known and is computer referenced to create a triangulation point.

Radio waves and their phasing are affected by a number of factors. For example, they alter in forward velocity every time they cross a land/sea boundary, so if your signal passes over several headlands and islands to reach your antenna, it will be distorted and give a slightly inaccurate distance from aerial to source. Much the same happens because of the night and day effect of the shifting ionospheric layer about 200km above the Earth's surface and from which radio signals bounce. A simple diagram illustrates this effect. The angle of incidence is equal to the angle of reflection — ie input and reflected output angles are the same, so the signals go further when the ionosphere is higher. This brings them to the aerial at a different angle and at a different velocity, which also causes distortion. The ionised layer also absorbs some signal and even refuses to reflect certain components, according to its density at the time.

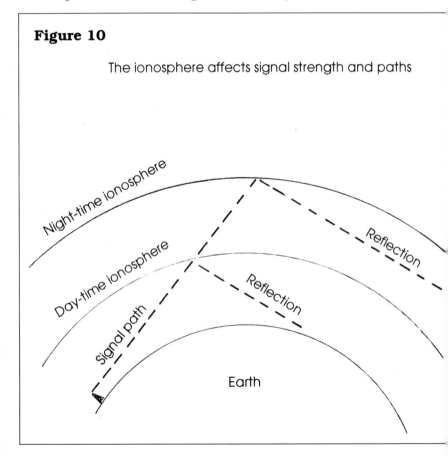

Figure 10

The ionosphere affects signal strength and paths

Land signals are also affected by the season and by the weather. All seafarers have seen radio conditions deteriorate in winter and anybody who has ever owned a normal domestic, or car radio will have experienced the signal-polluting effects of static and other electrical noise. The frequency band of land based radio navigational methods can also be easily deliberately jammed and distorted by badly intentioned outside influences.

Another limitation is the extent and the quality of the coverage, which combines with the phenomena above to impose constraints. Even in areas of northern Europe, which are supposed to be well covered by Decca and by Loran-C, a Decca receiver's reliability display will often show a circle of uncertainty of over one and a half miles. This means that it can only say that you are somewhere in a circle of three miles diameter.

There are, unfortunately, many geographical areas which are not covered by Decca or Loran-C. Southern Britain has been badly served by Loran-C and many popular areas of the Mediterranean have no Decca coverage. There is no Decca in the United States and no Loran-C in many parts of Europe other than those already mentioned above. Some traffic areas have neither. In our own experience we have crossed the Bay of Biscay several times and received good signals from the British Decca chain until we were sixty miles clear of the French coast, then ran on dead reckoning, beneath skies generally too cloudy to permit a sextant shot, until we were about sixty miles from the Iberian coast and the Spanish Decca transmitters became accessible.

In its pure form, GPS suffers none of these seasonal, climatological, nationalistic, nor geographic limitations. Left as the scientists and engineers designed it, GPS is capable of giving a position fix to a ten to fifteen metre accuracy with good reliability to very ordinary receivers. Furthermore, it will give this precise information irrespective of time of day, season, weather and where you happen to be — on land, on the sea or in the air.

With good equipment and by taking a few extra pre-cautions, people like surveyors and others using GPS aerials which are stationary, can get positional data and distances from other fixed points, accurate to just a few centimetres.

This precision is denied to the rest of us by a number of selfish political, economic and nationalistic factors. The main bogey is Selective Availability.

The GPS satellites belong to the United States Department of Defense. It was a very costly system to research and develop and also very expensive to launch via the Cape Kennedy rocket and space programme. It also needs on-going money to maintain the monitor and control stations.

As we briefly discussed in the introduction, the American government only sanctioned this huge budget on condition that such a super system's transport and safety benefits could be made available to a usage wider than purely military applications. This sent shivers of apprehension down the spines of the generals. There were fears that terrorists and foreign powers could very easily get access to the system and deliver explosive hardware with the same frightening precision enjoyed by US forces themselves. There was also a touch of civilian apprehension that if a merchant ship was relying on GPS and this had to be switched at the satellite end, there could be a legal wrangle about responsibility for an accident. Even though a compensation claim might have doubtful validity, it would still create embarrassing waves.

The decided solution was to give civilians access to a less precise signal than that used by the military. This was not a very big inconvenience to the planners, because two levels of precision and reliability had already been incorporated in the design.

This duality was necessary because of the very high accuracy criteria specified by the military, who wished to make their rockets hit particular parts of a ship and to get their 'smart' bombs guided down enemy ventilation shafts. Their ability to do this was well demonstrated and publicised during the Gulf War.

In order to achieve this phenomenal precision, the GPS receivers in the hardware need reference signals of extremely high purity and reliability. To achieve this and to allow receivers to lock on to the satellites very quickly even after the military vehicles have been moved a couple of thousand miles, two levels of satellite signal access code are needed.

The principal military frequency transmits its signals encrypted in P-Code, which stands for Precision. This is capable of giving unassisted accuracies better than ten metres, but in order to achieve this and to prevent blocking and access by third parties, the P-Code is incredibly complex and constantly changing. Only a specifically programmed receiver is able to unscramble and to use these signals. A side-effect is that even military equipment needs to know approximately where it is in order to lock on to these very finely tuned transmissions. For this reason, the satellites also send out a C-Code (Coarse Acquisition) on a different frequency. This is capable of fairly rapid lock-on, but its positional information is not as centimetre-precise as its more sophisticated companion.

The military decided to allow all civilians use of the C-Code whose frequencies, shifts and protocols were made available in the public domain. Contrary to common opinion, the C, or C/A-Code as it is sometimes called, has nothing to do with 'Civilian Access'. The fact that Coarse and Civilian have the same initial letter is merely coincidental.

It was a bit unfortunate for the generals and admirals, that the companies who began to design and manufacture hardware for non-military use did their job so well, that their receivers using the C-Code were giving accuracies better than ten metres for most of the time and better than fifteen metres all of the time. This should not have come as too much of a surprise, because the huge American and Americano-Japanese companies who had been engaged in all the pioneering work on military contracts were quick to see and to seize the vast financial rewards certain to accrue when GPS was released to the public. They had learned much from developing GPS and all this experience and error-free knowledge was poured out in order to attract the big money their way.

Because the civilian accuracy was about ten times greater than the military had expected, all their apprehensions began to return again. They delayed doing anything about them because they were, at this time, embroiled in the Gulf War and suffering from a shortage of khaki coloured GPS receivers for their radar controlled guns, rockets, aircraft and vehicles. Luckily, they were able to turn to a very efficient non-military market, which was just bringing some really superb GPS equipment off the production line. For a time, we leisure users were almost unable to purchase GPS gear, but there was plenty of Trimble, JRC, Garmin and Raytheon to be found in tanks patrolling the sands of Araby.

For the civilian user already equipped with GPS, this was a very good time. During the conflict, we made a GPS and radar passage between Ushant and Brittany down through the notorious Chenal du Four and through the Raz de Sein in visibility of less than fifty metres. All the buoys and towers came up within a few metres of where they should be and any discrepancy was probably because the paper chart could not match the electronic precision. It was very safe and comforting to pilot the yacht to within a few feet of the La Plate tower and turn the corner towards Audierne and the feeling certainly removed some of our worries about crossing Biscay.

Alas, those halcyon days were short-lived. Once the problems of Iraq had been resolved, the military minds returned to the lucky civilian and his present ability to match military position fixing precision. Their solution was to introduce into the C/A code a polluting element to reduce its pure precision. This Selective Availability (S/A) addition makes the satellite atomic clock tell small fibs about the time that a signal segment was transmitted. We are only talking about a very small fraction of a second, but this is enough to open out an ever-changing circle of uncertainty, not large enough to make GPS unusable, or even dangerous to civilian users, but sufficient to create in his mind doubts about exactitude and totally precise reliability.

This obviously begets the question 'Just how accurate is GPS in its civilian form?'

Perhaps we should begin by asking just how accurate is any part of current navigational data and competence. Many Admiralty charts rely on surveys done fifty and more years ago using equipment far less sophisticated than we now have. The Hydrographer will only guarantee many charts to 0.10 nm — or about 200 metres. Are you sure that your hand-bearing compass is perfectly accurate, or that the user's eye is properly aligned when he calls out the bearing? A Decca unit might show a lobster pot to be 300 metres from a headland when its real position is 250 metres from this same datum point. As long as the fisherman can return to his floating marker, he considers his Decca to be accurate.

So in talking of accuracy, what is our yardstick? To what can be compare the present precision level of GPS in order to get a valid picture of its use to civilians?

About the only sure way is to stand a GPS unit on such a very precise location such as a trigonometrical point, clear of all obstructions to a 360 degree horizon and not near any sources of electrical interference like power cables and units using three-phase current. Then you need to plot the displayed position over a sufficient period of time to produce some reliable averages, which take into account things like the very tiny errors caused by factors already discussed and which might actually cancel out a S/A error and so on.

The most reliable, generally accepted method for quoting averages is Root Mean Square (rms) terminology. It is defined as the square root of the average of the squares of a set of numbers, quantities or qualities. For example the rms of — say — the three values 1 - 2 - 4 would be the square root of the figures above (all to the power two) divided by three. This equals seven.

In GPS language, its accuracy is said to be of the order of two drms. In practical layman's language this means that about 65% of the fixes will be within 50 metres of the actual position and 95% of the displayed positions will be within 100 metres of your precise locations.

As a practical navigator, using GPS in numerous locations pretty well every day for about six months of the year, I always opt for the worst scenario that the boat is somewhere inside a circle measuring 200 metres across its diameter. Out in the open sea, anywhere in the world, to know where I am to within 100 metres radius come day, night, fog or hail is pretty phenomenal. Closer to shore, I expect to be able to quantify the GPS accuracy more precisely by reference to some other factor — a landmark, a buoy, an echo sounder reading, the radar and my eyes.

Even there, that still makes GPS a pretty phenomenal pilotage and safety tool, whose practical passage-making applications we shall return to when we describe a specimen, tutorial voyage using its wizardry. For the moment we can offer a comparative summary of GPS with its terrestrial radio position fixing competitors Decca and Loran-C by saying that even with S/A switched on, as far as a first fix is concerned it is as good as either of them when they are operating under their best possible conditions and very much better than either of them at their worst.

GDOP OR HDOP

A ship-board GPS display will also sometimes show an uncertain position fix because of what is generally called Geometric Dilution of Position(GDOP), or occasionally Horizontal Dilution of Position (HDOP) both of which are pretty good descriptive terms for an aberration which rarely lasts very long.

A few quick sketches and observations will soon show that some reference angles (or satellite positions) are more likely than others to give a precise fix point. We must also take into account signal width. For example, if you are given a position supposedly calculated to three decimal places, the final digit represents 0.001 nm or roughly six feet or 1.9 metres. On a large scale chart that would be less than the thickness of a mark on the chart made by the navigator's pencil, so we cannot work to such a tolerance.

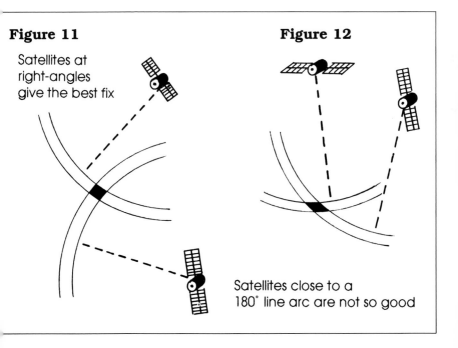

Figure 11

Satellites at right-angles give the best fix

Figure 12

Satellites close to a 180° line arc are not so good

Now imagine such lines projected from two satellites placed at ninety degrees to each other, which would give us a position somewhere inside a small box whose corners are the edges of the square formed by the thickness of the pencil lines (Fig 11). If the angle between our satellites increases by moving them closer to being 180 degrees, or tending towards being on a straight line, our thickness square gets bigger and also alters shape to become more like a diamond. We still know that we are somewhere inside the box, but it is a bigger horizontal box because the geometric disposition of the satellites being used is not good (Fig 12).

Most GPS receivers sound a warning when the position fix error oversteps the in-built tolerances because the GDOP or HDOP, which is more generally used in two-dimensional lat/long applications, is too high for reliability. The most sophisticated (and the most expensive) receiver in our own boat's GPS armoury has one display screen dedicated to HDOP. It calculates how much the position fix error magnifies from zero to ten and warns when the graph reaches six. At any moment, I can call up that page to see a history of the HDOP over the previous twenty-four hours, which generally shows magnifications in the two to three range.

Figure 13

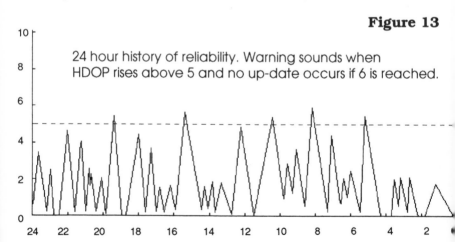

24 hour history of reliability. Warning sounds when HDOP rises above 5 and no up-date occurs if 6 is reached.

The GDOP/HDOP phenomenon has been described in some detail because it exists. In round terms, the lower the HDOP, the better the fix. Fortunately, because there are plenty of transmitter birds flying and they are constantly on the move, a poor alignment (high HDOP) is not very frequent and rarely lasts long. Even then, it is often likely to be more the fault of where the boat is situated at the time than of any inherent shortcoming in the receiver.

For example, our own most frequent experience of HDOP alarm occurred in a season cruising the rias — those narrow fjords which run deep between the tall hills of Galicia and the other provinces of north-west Spain. Our six channel GPS unit is normally tracking five or six satellites and selecting the best three for a position fix — best here means that they have an acceptable height above the horizon and that they are at three angles small enough to give a small cocked hat. Often the most useful satellites were hidden behind the mountains and our poor old machine was being asked to calculate from very second choice reference signals.

Out in the clear, the irritant of high HDOP is comparatively rare and never of worrying duration.

In many ways, this chapter has indulged the conservatism of discussing worst possible scenarios. If it has seemed to diminish admiration: forget it. I am a big fan of GPS and would never want to go to sea without it. Even after several years of heavy usage, I have still not lost my sense of wonder at how it works. Because, under another recreational hat, I am a licensed radio amateur, I have a comprehension feeling for the signal reception part of GPS equipment, but I am still bewildered and fascinated by the very rapid way in which it can plot two positions and then project the line between them to give me a score of useful navigational facts about distance, relative position of hazards, speed, course to steer and several interpretations of time.

Could a navigator possibly ask for more?

Chapter 4

Choosing the Equipment

Buying a GPS receiver is not something which can be done with the easy simplicity of purchasing an electric plug or a shackle. The market explosion which has followed the availability of such a versatile and ubiquitous system has inspired many producers to rush new equipment onto the market whilst the cash-bearing customers are still hungrily scouring the market place. Amongst the excellent gear in the chandlers' catalogues, there is also — and alas inevitably — a vast amount of rubbish, sometimes purveyed by salesmen who are less than honest in their advice about suitability and often being described and promoted by people who have scant understanding of how GPS works in practice.

Even when considering well-designed and well-engineered GPS receivers, it should be realised that not all products are suitable for all applications, so the purchaser needs to do some research to avoid disappointment and wasting money. The classic illustration of this advice is an acquaintance who bought a hand-held GPS receiver for an archeological expedition to northern Scotland. He was persuaded into a unit reading out in latitude and longitude and thereafter doing some complicated arithmetic, simply because the salesman was not aware that some companies produce receivers which display position as six-figure National Grid references. On site, the integral rechargeable NiCad battery gave up the ghost after a couple of hours use, which did not please a group of people searching for their point of interest in a location far away from habitations and with no possibility of finding an electricity supply to recharge their troublesome battery.

Being a careful buyer begins with the analysis of what you expect your GPS receiver to do and where both the display and the antenna will be mounted — hand, car, boat, aircraft and bicycle have all been equipped.

The next consideration is what actual space is available for installation. Are you looking for a unit to mount on a console and is it to be surface-mounted or flush-fitted? Perhaps you need it to be on a trunnion or a U-bracket fixed to a shelf, or even suspended beneath it. If it is on an open boat, should you be looking for a completely waterproof specification? Then you need to sort out the power supply and its route for permanence, recharging or easy removal of the unit for security.

Against these basic practical criteria, you should also be asking yourself how much use you will be getting from the new equipment and how much precision you really need. How large should/must your budget be to get value for money? Are you looking for simple, stand-alone three-function navigation (position-store, bearing-to-waypoint, distance-to-waypoint) or might you want extra information with perhaps the ability to interface your GPS with a chart plotter and a multi-function repeater on a flybridge, or at a yacht's wheel?

All these things are possible, but they are not all available in all pieces of equipment. Our own system is to write a list of essential and desirable functions and to mark them with an 'essentiality' or a 'desirability' percentage. Storing latitude/longitude co-ordinates gets 100%, as do bearing-and-distance to waypoint. A route-store and an indication of cross-track error rates 90%, speed-over-ground gets 70%, but we only rate 40% or less for a read-out to three decimal places.

When we have agreed our budget, we then go looking at receivers which satisfy all our physical criteria, but also have the most 100% and near 100% functions on our list. This method of narrowing down the selection from the ninety-plus GPS units currently on the market has worked well for us, even though our two current boats probably represent the extreme poles of decision. Our dive-boat is a thirty-five knot open RIB with an outboard, but for six months of the year we live and work on a ten-metre motor-sailer with a totally enclosed wheelhouse, plenty of electronic accessories and a top speed of eight knots.

Once you have a basis for choice, you must remember that a GPS navigator is a mixture of radio receiver and computer. There is a broad overlap between the functions of the two and they are often lumped together under the term 'Channel'. Generally, the more channels a unit boasts, the faster it will work and certain elements of its data output will be more accurate and smoother — ie the readings will not jump about as much. These multi-channel receivers are mostly more expensive. Although in practice, all GPS receivers work adequately well, this is one area of electronic life where the quality you get is directly proportional to what you pay.

There is an ascending ladder of price and efficiency.

Single Channel
Single channel receivers are exactly as the name suggests. They have just one central receiving and processing device which handles the received time signals and the other radio data, but regularly has to turn away from this task in order to process the received information into the angles, the running times and the distances a navigator requires for safe pilotage.

Such receivers are usually physically small with an LCD display of meagre dimensions and low luminosity contrast. There is less circuitry — but this consumes less power — and the clock is not always of the best quality. The single channel receiver cannot constantly monitor a galaxy of several satellites, so it looks at them in turn and then makes averaging assumptions about boat speed and direction. This can give rise to a very jumpy display of information.

Multiplexer Receivers
These are really single channel units with a more flashy name and a bit of extra computing memory and power to do all the number crunching more rapidly. They are sometimes given confusing names like 'Fast Multiplexer' and the brochures do not always confess that you are still only getting one receive channel.

This particular system has now become so complex that the prices have crept up to be quite close to those charged for a machine with several full receiving channels. It is worth doing a bit of comparative research here.

Because a single channel, or single channel multiplex GPS unit, requires relatively little current, this is the system usually adopted for hand-held, or hand-portable equipment. They are sometimes called 'starved receivers' because of this and because some of them close-down voltage gobbling back-lit displays if no button has been pushed for a set period of time. As long as the antenna can still see the satellites, it will continue to up-date the unit's position and to compute distances, bearings and travel times to destinations, but if it is in your pocket, you may have to wait a couple of minutes for it to lock on to the signals again when you next come to use it.

Two-Channel Sequencing GPS
This type of receiver has not continued in favour, even though they make sense for some applications. They are better all round performers than single channelers because one slot can be processing the data, whilst the other is hunting for and then receiving the next satellite. (To do this takes about one thousandth of the time which it takes to tell.) The second channel doubles the available random code amplification, so a two-channel unit has better signal-to-noise ratios and a firmer display because of it. Users will also notice that the read-out of speed will be less inclined to jump about.

Multi-Channel Receivers
Multi-Channel receivers are unarguably better than any other alternatives as long as you have the physical space and budget capacities to cope. There are three, four, five, six and twelve and then even twenty-four channel models in production and the range has quite surprising and very practical poles of size and price. However, the rules about quality and cost still apply.

Multi-channels bring multi advantages. One of the most noticeable is that even if you are in undulating terrain, or your antenna is screened by another boat, or a building, an alarm indicating high GDOP or HDOP is quite rare. Instead of missing, or totally ignoring a position update because the single computer is doing something else, the multi-channel receiver is monitoring more satellites. So, even if the ephemeris almanac reckons that — say — Satellite 10 is the best transmitter currently available in good conditions, but it is not visible because of an obstruction, another channel will lock on to something like Satellite 14, which is not in the ideal place, but will still be strong enough for a reliable position fix.

The increased signal-to-noise figures from six channels obviously also give more reliable readings and the extra computers mean that the speed of up-date is very rapid. This is most noticeable in the display of Speed-Over-Ground (Velocity) which is being continuously calculated, rather than averaged over several seconds. The multi-channels also run constant checks on each other and ignore any data which is far away from the rest because one channel has 'thrown a wobbler' for a fraction of a second.

On our own boat we have both single and multi-channel GPS units. The displayed speed of the former tends to jump around anywhere from 3.8 knots to 5.3 knots even when we are motoring in the calm tideless water of a canal and know that our velocity is 4.5 knots. The multi-channel receiver displays this correct speed most of the time, which means that its information is more reliable. This becomes important when you are 'tweaking' sails and want an immediate indication of the effect of the adjustment on boat speed.

Because they have the power, multi-channel receivers will usually have display screens which are large, brighter, carry more data in big digits and have better contrasting readability. The drawbacks are those of increased physical size, a bit more drain on batteries — not generally serious — and needing more cash to purchase — a matter of some import for many of us.

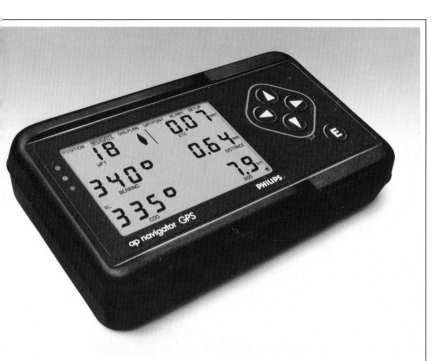

The Philips AP Mark 8 (above) is a good example of a multi-channel GPS receiver.

The single channel GPS 50 from Garmin International (left).

Obviously different GPS receivers have differing capabilities when it comes to using them as navigational tools and all navigators have different features and functions which they consider to be important. To clear the air, you will find outlined below the specifications and the functionality of two receivers, one which represents the lower end of the price range and the other almost the top. They have been selected because they are both good tools and both affordable by the non-commercial user.

There is little point in quoting names and addresses here because GPS technology is evolving so fast and there are so many takeovers and company realignment movements that information soon becomes out of date. We have no particular preference for any one particular make of equipment. The big companies advertising in the marine and aeronautical press all make good GPS receivers and you can buy these with the confidence of knowing that the supplier will still be there to service it in five years time and that you will be able to add the software improvements as they are developed.

So, in their separate ways and bearing in mind that some machines are more suitable than others for particular applications (such as our own two very different boats), there is plenty of choice.

Model A

Dimensions: 90 × 130 × 48 mm (3.5 × 5.1 × 1.9 inches)
Weight: 0.4kg (14oz)
Power: 12 or 24 v
Consumption: 1.3 Watts (without back-lighting)
Channels: multiplexer (tracking eight satellites)
Accuracy: 15 metres (2 drms)
Velocity: 90 knots
Interface: NMEA 0183
Display size: 55 × 45 mm (2.2 × 1.8 inches)
Display type: Low contrast LCD with large pixels

An example of a model 'A' type GPS receiver. It represents the cheaper end of the market and is therefore less sophisticated than the more expensive products.

The display size, type and its pixel count (more pixels equals better definition) are not quoted in the descriptive brochures and these are generally the give-away about the total quality of the machine, but it does only draw 0.18 amps.

Number of Waypoints: 250 with alpha or numeric description
Number of Routes: ten of twenty waypoints (reversible)

The sheer size of the memory is not really an indication of value. If you store 250 waypoints (WP) you would also need a separate paper list to keep track of them, but also remember that keeping too many WPs in the memory slows down the machine when you are programming it with a new passage and also alters the way in which it can be operated. Transferring them from memory to route on this machine is quite slow.

The route store is also cumbersome. A route of twenty WPs would be very complex to enter into memory and probably be confusing to use. Our own extensive cruising has never had a route needing more than ten WPs and the average is seven.

At switch-on Model A shows:

Satellite Bar Graph: The X axis plots the quality of the incoming signal on the scale 0—10 for the satellites which should be available and they are listed by their ID number along the horizontal Y axis. A marginally useful page.

Status Page: shows satellite ID number, its compass direction from True North, elevation above the horizon and signal strength. This is a very useful page, especially if the receiver is slow to lock on, or is sounding an alarm of no position up-date. From this display you could probably ascertain that the cause is poor HDOP rather than — for instance — an antenna or connection fault.

Satellite Sky View: is a simulated plan (helicopter view) representation of where each satellite is in relation to the antenna. As each is accessed it changes to reverse video.

This is a relatively useless page — clever graphics for the sake of electronic art rather than being of use to the user. The futility is aggravated by the small notchy screen and the information is seen better on other pages.

Auxiliary Page: is a computer style menu accessing the Set-Up functions allowing choice between such things as miles/kilometres, True/Magnetic compass, UTC/local time (Zulu or Alpha) and Map Datum (See section on accuracy).

Position Page: is an automatic display of present latitude and longitude in digits large enough to be easily read. The 'minutes' are in decimal notation to three places, which is entirely unnecessary and causes not only the third figure to dance confusingly, but also the second place to jump around when the .001 is at the top or bottom of a decade. This instability is greater on a multiplexer than it would be on a multi-channel GPS and makes the speed display even less steady. Track and speed are also shown when the boat is moving.

An essential page which could be better.

Waypoint Definition: This is the page where you enter WPs into the memory-store, or recall them from it for modification. The numerical components are entered from the keyboard and each can be given a five letter name, or text identifier. The actual typing-in operation is quite slow and each letter can need up to five keystrokes to bring up on the page. This protracts the time needed to program the machine prior to a voyage needing two or three routes of half a dozen waypoints each.

The longer you navigate, then the more you revert to a mixture of old skills and new techniques. Like many of my acquaintances, I have largely given up defining my WPs by names — which are often very shortened and difficult to remember a couple of months later. All my co-ordinate lists are kept in a book, usually in the order they were used. If they are still in memory it is quicker to recall them to screen by a couple of digits rather than by typing five letters, or by scrolling down a long list.

As I write, I am looking at a screen which says TRMPL and cannot for the life of me remember what the letters stand for without reference to my list, where it tell me that TRMPL is Trompeloupe lighthouse in the Gironde Estuary below Bordeaux. Having only five letters available leads to some very peculiar and often indecipherable abbreviations. On my list, Trompeloupe is number thirty-one and that makes a better and faster access delineator than the name shortened into GPS-speak.

Waypoint List: Simply a list of all the WPs in the memory bank. Unfortunately they are automatically sorted into alphabetical order, which is very clever and well-intentioned computer technology, but it does have a number of drawbacks.

If, for instance, I enter in a half a dozen WPs it is very likely that if they are needed again that I shall want to use them in roughly the same order, or even in reverse order to get home again. If these WPs have names like Alpha, Zulu, Mike, Bravo and Whisky, it is necessary to go chasing the cursor up and down the list to arrange them in that order and this takes time as well as leading to careless button pushing.

Model A has a route store, but it is not always convenient to keep data in this fashion — irrespective of model.

The 'Go To' button/page: A marvellous function which partly alleviates the WP selection traumata above. If the 'Go To' key is pushed when the cursor is over a particular place on the WP List screen, the course to steer to get to this place and the distance to it are immediately flashed up onto the screen and are soon joined by boat speed and time to get to destination.

If your journey is along a straight line to a single destination in store, one keystroke is the only programming necessary.

In our own case, if we are on a passage where we might pass close to rocks, wrecks or shallows, or even position-confirming buoys and lighthouses, we enter their co-ordinates into the memory. En route, if we ever wonder where we are in relation to one of these submerged hazards, or how far we are from the buoy which we have noted, a quick flip of the cursor to the right place on the screen menu and a touch on 'Go To' will tell us to calm down because the rock is still half a mile away and quite broad on the starboard bow.

'Go To' really is an excellent facility to have in order to speed up your navigation and to avoid the slips of parallel rules and pencil on a paper chart.

Navigate Pages: These are the ones which are most often used during a journey. Each one is a different combination of the factors which a navigator must consider. Basically, they allow you to choose a display of varied and varying data fields. The most often used screen shows, for example:

Thank you for buying this Waterline book. If you would like to be kept informed about our forthcoming publications, please fill in this card.

Name...

Address..

....

1) In order to assist our editors in determining the type of nautical books our readers require could you please tick your areas of interest in the spaces below.

Maritime History ☐   Cruising Handbooks ☐   Navigation & Meteorology ☐

Practical Seamanship ☐   Boatbuilding & Design ☐   Boat Maintenance & Repair ☐

2) How did this book come to your notice?

☐ Magazine Advertisement. Which magazine? _____

☐ Book Review. Which publication? _____

☐ In a bookshop. Which bookshop?. _____

3) In which Waterline book did you find this card? _____
(Please specify title)

WATERLINE
101 LONGDEN ROAD
SHREWSBURY
SHROPSHIRE SY3 9BR
GREAT BRITAIN

BRG 109 — bearing to waypoint

RNG 14.7 — range, or distance, to WP

COG 155 — course over ground

SOG 5.7 — speed over ground

XTE 0.8 — cross-track error distance and direction

These pages are excellently thought out and a really good navigational tool.

Plotter Pages: On Model A these are — again — clever graphics but are navigationally useless, partly because of the lack of fine definition clarity in the small, notchy screen and also because they do not tell you anything which you really need to know.

Screen One: has the representation of the boat's track with lines getting closer together, like making a drawing of a straight road or a railway track running away from you, as they go from bottom to top of the screen. In theory, the marker showing the boat's position can be kept in the middle of this track a bit like an arcade computer game. If you stray from centre it shows.

In practice it is impossible to use — yes, because of screen quality, but also because constantly changing Selective Availability errors cause the cursor to jump about the screen too much for reliability or accuracy.

Plotter Screen Two: is even worse. It is a North-Up representation of an area of the sea, or sky onto which the boat's track history over a selectable time span and map scale is shown. The pixels on the screen are so large in relation to the distances involved that even the straightest course-keeping comes out like a zigzag on the screen. It also has to be pointed out that with no chart overlay, or any other factor against which the plotted position can be referenced, the whole exercise is pretty pointless, even for a sailing-boat skipper who might be interested in a visual record of leeway and pinching angles. This is a page I never use.

In conclusion, the person who buys Model A at the current price is in no sense being ripped off. He is getting what he paid for and must accept the limitation of the graphics on the small screen and sometimes the irritations of single-channel receiver inconsistency. Having said that, I should have no apprehension about navigating from England to the Mediterranean with Model A as my main position-fixing tool. Plenty of people have done it — including ourselves.

Model B

Model B is a top of the range, top of the price mountain, full six-channel GPS receiver costing over four times the price of Model A but, for serious navigators, having more than four times the possible application. Model B has obviously been designed by serious navigators with long term practical navigation in mind and this shows as soon as you get it out of the box and open up the operating manual.

Dimensions: 300 × 150 × 67 mm (11.8 × 5.9 × 2.6 inches)

Weight: 1.2 kg (2.65 lb)

Power: 12v – 24v

Consumption: 7.0 w Max.

Channels: Six

Accuracy: 0.1 m/sec

Frequency: 1575.42 MHz

Interface: NMEA 0183

Display Size: 136 × 70 mm (5.4 × 2.75 inches) approx

Display Type: High contrast back-lit LCD with high resolution of lines per millimetre (small pixels) and reverse video for easy night-time viewing.

The GPS Mark 6 Navigator from Philips Navigation AS, is an example of a model 'B' type. Note the large, clear display screen.

The dimensions show this to be a large, heavily engineered unit designed to stand up to a rough life at sea and having a screen whose displayed digits and graphics can be seen from the other side of the wheelhouse, even by that 35% of the world's population who normally wear spectacles for reading. The bigger size also connotes much easier installation and ease of repair at sea if a cable jumps off. This would be unlikely because Model B's published specification quotes meeting very rigid standards for vibration, heat, cold etc and every unit is tested for seventy-two hours in changing environments before it is packed for despatch.

Apart from the space needed to mount the display and having a slightly bulkier antenna, the down side is that Model B's six channels and very bright screen are rated to seven watts or 0.6 amps — not serious but high in comparison with many other GPS receivers. You are, however, getting a lot for your current.

Figure 17

© SAILPLAN 1	SAILPLAN	
Remaining to end: 304Nm / 7WPTs	ETA 09:11 Sun 4 Nov	Direction ↓
70	PT.JULECK SW	04:05 Fri 2 Nov	
71	PT.JULECK NW	08:37 Fri 2 Nov	31.1Nm 35°
72	NUMAN ISL. E	17:06 Fri 2 Nov	62.1Nm 161°
73	SEAGULL RF SE	14:23 Sat 3 Nov	145Nm 199°

The AP VI Electronic Ship's Log.

Sailplan 2: The co-ordinates, waypoints and Marks of Special interest are entered into the Sailplan Two memory by buttons large enough and sufficiently widely spaced to permit use even when you are wearing gloves. The separate sites are listed sequentially as you enter their latitude and longitude, but there is also a space alongside for the addition of two lines of descriptive text, or a name, which could be up to forty characters. The software also offers very clear graphic symbols which can be inserted as aides memoires. Those depicting port and starboard channel buoys and the four cardinal marks are particularly useful.

The last twenty slots of the two-hundred Waypoint (WP) memory bank are reserved for immediate position store. If, for example, a fisherman observes an interesting patch of sea bottom on the video sounder, a single keystroke will record its co-ordinates and the time it was logged. The other data can be added at leisure.

Sailplan 3: This is a twenty unit route store, rapidly created by keying in the points in any order and this can be changed, or extra WPs inserted very easily and at any time. The route can be made to work in either direction and can be lifted in toto and 'dumped' into the page controlling the day's passage or work, where it can stand alone, or be amalgamated with other data. Whichever entry mode is selected, the distance between waypoints and the course to steer between them is immediately calculated and displayed.

Sailplan 1: A very well designed electronic log. The basis is a sailing plan of the route written to screen by keying in the simple WP numbers from the sequential master list. The Point of Departure and the time of leaving are automatically put onto the top line as soon as the GPS receiver senses that the boat is moving. A single button push toggles the actual WP data display between lat/long co-ordinates, or the descriptive name text for writing the Ship's log etc. (Fig 17)

Figure 18

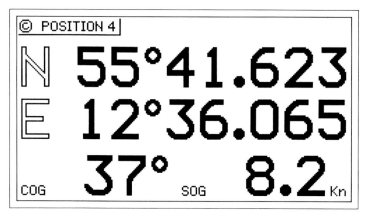

Information large enough for easy reading.

A super feature of this page is that every time a WP is passed, the time and date are automatically recorded and that section of the display changes from black on white to reverse video and the display of remaining distances (to next wp and the end of the route) also continue to change. It often happens that the skipper is busy doing other things as the WP is passed, but he can write up the Ship's log from the electronic data at the end of the day.

The actual WP pass time recorded depends on operator choice. It is only rarely that a passage maker will pass over the exact spot of the co-ordinates. The boat can be pushed sideways by the tide, or the skipper might decide to cut a corner. Model B offers four methods of marking the pass time. They are:

A: when you enter a specified circle drawn around the WP

B: when you cross an imaginary line through the WP and perpendicular to the present course

C: when you cross an imaginary line bisecting the present course line and the next leg of the route

D: (the default selection) when you cross an imaginary line bisecting the angle drawn by present course and next leg. The software automatically differentiates between acute and obtuse angles.

These choices are much more clearly seen from the illustration than from words and selection is quick and simple. It is part of the sophistication which the extra selling price conveys. (Fig 19)

Figure 19

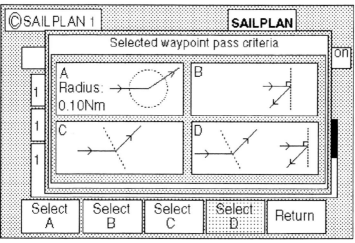

Navigate and Position Keys
The 'Navigate' and 'Position' keys and their associated displays have a degree of overlap but comprise half a dozen different screens allowing a wide variety of possible methods of viewing the normally required position fixing and boat progress information. This is :-

Position in latitude and longitude	XTE distance
Bearing to next WP	Name/number of next WP
Distance to next WP	Time to reach next WP
Course Over Ground (COG)	Time to end of route
	Clock time at both of these
Speed Over Ground (SOG)	Present time in UTC (GMT) and local time
Cross-Track Error (XTE) direction.	Graphic indicator of XTE

This wealth and variety of data is a real navigator's friend and is — again — what your extra money brings. It means that you can select a crowded screen displaying plenty of information, which is being up-dated every second, or alternatively opt for one showing the position in figures large enough to be legible from several feet away. The graphic showing a boat outline indicating the distance off track and the direction to steer to get back on course is clear enough to be usable, thanks to the big screen and its fine lines.

Model B has many other functions and displays for time alarms, malfunction alarms, chronometers, security lock against unauthorised use and some really practical pages giving ephemeris and almanac information of satellite angle, elevation and signal strength and a graph and graphic display of twenty-four hour HDOP history. There is also plenty of choice of chart datum points and selection of which NMEA sentences you wish the receiver to output to other devices.

This is all very sophisticated and extremely useful — there are no wasted and unnecessary functions and displays, whilst the menus are arranged so clearly that even such a mass of data and computing is easy to understand and to use. Part of the high price is because it is easy to understand and to use and also the intensive and successful research and development. Amongst it, there are two extra displays worthy of special mention.

The unit contains three distance logs. The first records miles, nautical miles or kilometres (easy select) since the unit was installed. This can only be set at the factory, but there are also two resetable logs. You could, for instance, use one to record the season's mileage and use the other for each day's route, or to get an accurate measurement of the distance between two intermediate points on a log.

Plotter Screens

As we touched on earlier, many GPS unit screen plotters are relatively useless because of small screens, notchy pixel display and the inconsistencies of single-channel lack of smoothness. Model B has a couple of plotter and track history screens enabled by the opposite of the three deterrents above.

Plotter one is particularly useful. It is a North-Up display covering an area variable from one to one hundred and twenty miles. The XTE limits before a warning sounds, can be set and rapidly altered by the user at any time and are displayed as parallel lines on the screen, which also puts up all the WPs as flag markers. En route, the boat icon remains in the centre of the screen, but pivots to show in which direction it is travelling relative to desired course. The other display factors scroll over this icon, but a fine line track history is also recorded. All the other normal data is shown in a screen edge panel. (Fig. 20)

Figure 20

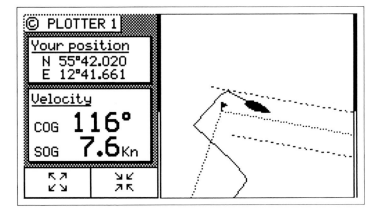

This one plotter screen alone completely converted a doubting skipper to the virtues of modern electronics, when he was making a four-day crossing of the Bay of Biscay with a relatively inexperienced crew. When he wanted to get some sleep, he was able to set Plotter One's XTE lines to one nm either side of the rhumb line course between his WPs spaced twenty miles apart from Ushant to Cabo Prior.

The helmsman on watch was instructed to keep an eye on the boat's position between the XTE lines. If it moved out towards a XTE limit line, the autopilot could be adjusted a couple of degrees to bring her back to the centre. If she crossed the limit line, the skipper was to be called.

Hand-held GPS Receivers

The observant will have noticed that we have made no mention of hand-held GPS receivers whilst discussing the criteria for choice of equipment. It is acknowledged that the technology in hand-portable GPS is excellent, but a unit which cannot be bolted to something fixed, has no place on a boat as mainstream navigational equipment. Additionally, because the antenna needs to see a clear sky for best efficiency, the GPS receiver is best served by an external, permanently mounted antenna. Some portable units offer this, but when you add its cost, the bill comes to much the same as that for a proper marine instrument with a better screen.

There are some GPS models which are described as portable rather than hand-held. These can be taken home for secure storage, but this also applies to very expensive GPS units like Model B, already described, which are merely lifted off the bracket, leaving all the connections in situ.

So, to go out again via the door we used to come in, we must remind ourselves that the Global Positioning System is an incredible technical achievement, which is made available to us totally free of charge but there are diminutions of function inherent in the design of particular receivers.

Chapter 5

Evaluating GPS Equipment

The Global Positioning System is a bit like cars and computers in that you do not need to understand them completely in order to drive them, but the operator who knows a little about the background principles and something about how they are translated into displayed information will get much more satisfaction, personal efficiency and safety from them. To the last chapter's evaluation of what appears on the screen, we should now add a few more details of how it gets there.

Such knowledge is interesting in its own right, but it also enables the prudent buyer to ask enough sharp questions to read between the lines of brochure hyperbole and to see beyond the salesmen's eulogy of equipment which they have perhaps never used under real conditions and which — in all honesty — they often understand far less than they pretend.

If you have a basic comprehension of the physical and engineering principles involved, you can make your own evaluation of a GPS receiver, even before you reach for your cheque book, or fit it to your boat.

It would be a rare dealer indeed who would let you borrow a GPS unit for testing, but we have known some main agents willing to let their demonstration models be put through the hoop. You may even know an owner of one of the models on your short list and could persuade him to do some practical evaluation with you, whilst the receiver is off the boat for the winter.

A dealer's showroom is absolutely the last place to attempt a practical evaluation of any GPS unit. The microwave signals coming from the satellites are capable of passing through walls, but they suffer very significant attenuation (weakening) in the process. In some locations they will also be disturbed by interference from heavy industrial electricity supply, thermostat harmonics and even from noise generated by shop tills, door alarms and television videos. This same internal location can also create weird time/phase distortion effects, when a signal bounces off several different radio reflective layers and arrives by a devious route and from an incorrect direction. This could falsify the time apparently taken for the signal to travel from satellite to antenna. As we have already seen, GPS accuracy is totally dependent on time and even a very small chronological discrepancy can create a significant distance error.

If a position fix is only as good as its reception of signals, we must also take into account that the signals themselves are only as good as the antenna. In dealing with radios (even GPS radios) the amateur first looks at the display box, whereas the professional's first inspection is of the aerial. Radio quality is entirely dependent on aerial efficiency. If you purchase a £2,000 radio and try to capture its signals with a £2 aerial, you are using a £2 radio. GPS receivers also follow this rule.

Antenna efficiency is governed by two factors
(a) the design and engineering of the antenna
(b) where the antenna is sited.

Factor (a) can safely be left to the GPS designers as long as you are buying a receiver which has been specifically produced for the medium you occupy — sea or air. To be effective, your GPS receiver must have a dedicated external antenna, which can satisfy criterion (b) by being sited out in the clear, where — if possible — it has an uncluttered, 360° view of a horizon at sea level, ie it is not mounted so that is has a mast a few centimetres to one side and a 10 mm stainless-steel rigging wire almost touching the other. In practical terms, a boat GPS antenna will rarely achieve such perfection, but we must do the best we can.

Antenna height is not important. You mount your VHF aerial as high as possible so that it can have a good look over the curve of the horizon and to give it a better chance of 'seeing' a line of sight path to any other antenna with which it is working. Not so with GPS.

Satellite signals also travel line of sight, but because they are travelling down from space, they can see antennae with greater ease. There will be times when the hills around a Scottish loch, or the buildings adjacent to a quay will prevent the receiver from 'getting a good look at' a satellite, but the computer will usually manage to lock onto one in a less good, but adequate orbit.

When you look at your GPS unit's almanac display, you will see that the receiver generally first locks onto the satellites which are well above the horizon, because they are the ones sending down the strongest signals. Then it goes on to the weaker radiations. It is a mark of a best quality GPS design that the antenna and amplification circuits are sensitive enough to pick out these weaker ultra high frequency signals from all the millions of other waves always around us and so be able to use signal from satellites close to the horizon.

Because of the GPS signal's angle of approach, height has little to do with GPS antenna efficiency. It will work as well mounted on the guard rail or the cabin top as it will at the masthead. Indeed, the system is so sensitive that there are always very good reasons for not putting your antenna at the top of a 50-foot mast. Remember that your display is not giving the position of the black box and screen, but is giving the position of the top of the aerial. Imagine the length of arc transversed by the tip of that 50-foot pole rolling in a steep beam sea and you have a distance well able to confuse a sensitive receiver.

If the masthead is your only antenna-mounting possibility, you will be very badly served by some of the cheaper sets. Their position and speed displays will be very erratic. Expensive receivers contain a Kalman Filter (or something similar) whose software can be configured to take note of acceleration effects — including the gyrations of a tall mast. However, in spite of this possible technical solution, an aerial site less prone to swing will always be better — and probably less at risk from the hazards of the sea and air. If the antenna is accessible, there is some incentive to take it off before dropping the masts for winter storage. If it is at the masthead, we think twice about removal — and risk losing our no-claims bonus on equipment as the crane grabs the stick and lowers it to the deck.

In talking of vulnerability, the purchaser should be aware that there are several ways of constructing GPS receivers. If the unit is coming from an original equipment manufacturer, it is likely that almost all the sensitive circuitry will be protected inside the black box, safe and dry inside the cabin. The antenna will be fairly small, have low windage and contain little more than the receiving wire coil and a transmitter-driven pre-amplifier to give the signal a bit of a boost down the connecting cable.

The Apelco ANT 180 demonstrates just how compact GPS antennas have become.

Other systems put about 90% of the GPS circuitry, computers and clocks into an antenna pod. The give-away is the size of this equipment which is designed to be used by companies who do not themselves manufac-turer GPS receivers but wish to incorporate the GPS facility into — say — a chart plotter, or to feed the signal into an on-board data box for passing on to their own display units.

There is a fair amount of this sort of equipment about and it works well enough because the antenna is almost a complete GPS unit in its own right, but there are a number of reasons why it has not found favour in our own purchases.

Firstly, I much prefer integrated systems where every-thing comes from one source and is assembled in house. It tends to be less messy than 'mix and match' systems and in the event of something going wrong the resident engineers generally know the equipment well enough to complete an on-the-spot repair, or to give useful informa-tion on the telephone. I am also not enamoured of bulky, high windage aerials which — logically — must be more susceptible to damage.

My heart and wallet really ached for the owner of a yacht we saw at Roscoff. Whilst he was shopping, a fishing boat berthed alongside him and the dropping tide caused the two boats to lean in towards each other as they took the ground. The trawler's lobster pot hoisting gear snapped off the yacht's bulky GPS antenna, for which the replacement cost was £700 plus a hefty car-riage bill and a long wait for the new antenna to be deliv-ered.

Luckily, our own slender, dedicated GPS antenna escaped when a badly moored small crabber boat came forward on its mooring warps and hit our davits where the aerials are mounted. Had they been damaged, replacement would have cost no more than £100, but the insides of these particular aerials are so simple that we would probably have been able to make the repair with a bit of careful soldering.

The discussion of the importance of antennae etc must also shed light on the limitation of the breed of small hand-portable GPS units currently flooding onto the market. For many applications they are not good, simply because even in GPS life a good big one will always beat a good little one of the same species. This shows clearly in our previous chapter's comparison of big Model B and small Model A, which would itself out-perform most hand-held units.

In the nature of any pocketable item there is less physical space for a clear screen, legible graphics and long battery life. The integral antenna can only see a full and clear horizon if the whole unit is held up in the clear, which usually means taking it outside the cabin and holding the entire receiver where it is not screened by your body. There is nothing technically inferior about hand-portable GPS units when seen against equipment of equivalent specification re number of channels etc. However, on boats and aboard aircraft, where the display is surrounded by walls and electrical interference and (it bears repeating) an external antenna is essential, we should perhaps question the wisdom of purchasing a GPS unit which has an integral aerial and which can fall off ledges, be sat upon and even disappear into pockets other than those of the rightful owners. There are better solutions at similar prices.

It has been interesting to note that even since we began researching this book, many manufacturers of hand-held GPS units are now supplying a fixing bracket as an optional extra. They have obviously seen the light. How long before they also offer an external antenna kit? Then, what will be the difference between a hand-portable (portability apart) and a larger, clearer fixed ship or aircraft unit?

These are all factors to be borne in mind when you are contemplating purchase and set out to 'road test' a GPS receiver. This is an ideal description, because a car and an open space like an airfield perimeter track, or a motor-racing circuit make an ideal test combination, especially if you can either gutter-mount the antenna, or fix it to the centre of the roof with temporary adhesive, or a radio ham style magnetic mount.

Many airfields have a marker stone sited at a very precisely known location, which will probably be in that country's national survey six-figure grid reference numbers. Some GPS units have this built in, but it is no problem to convert to latitude and longitude to a different matrix format. You may even be able to park next to a Trigonometrical Point which will act as a reference to check the basic GPS accuracy.

In normal circumstances, you should not have any serious discrepancy here because, under controlled (static) conditions, most models will give a satisfactory position fix. You are more interested in stability of readout. We should not forget that Selective Availability causes the position to shift around within the 200-metre diameter circle of uncertainty, but this is not a constant movement. Here we are just having a look at the quality of the machine which — in the general terms we have already discussed — is indicated by display stability.

It would be very poor test procedure to try to verify basic accuracy by reference to features on a marine chart. As part of our professional life we once fielded a very irate lady passed to us as independent observers by a manufacturer. She was telephoning from Brittany to complain that her newly purchased GPS was totally inaccurate. Questioning revealed that she was taking as her yardstick the position of a buoy called 'La Grande Basse de Portsall', which was created to keep inshore vessels clear of the wreck of the *Amoco Cadiz* on the rocky corner of Brittany. The lady's co-ordinates had been extrapolated from the Admiralty Chart of the area.

If we ignore that cartographers do not specifically guarantee the absolute precision of the symbols on charts and if we add a number of interpretative and print-slip possibilities, we soon see that this was a nonsense of a reference point. The water depth at Portsall is forty-three metres at Lowest Astronomical Tide and the tidal range at Springs is eight metres on top of this. The buoyage engineers also add at least another extra twenty metres of chain to cope with the big waves at this notorious place. This means that our lady's reference point was moving up and down the Channel according to the tide on over seventy metres of chain. It was asking a bit much to use it to check the precision of a sophisticated electronic device which can give fifteen metres accuracy.

It was also interesting to note that my lat/long taken from the chart did not exactly agree with the complainant's version and neither of us coincided with the position quoted in the excellent Bloc Marine almanac *Votre Livre de Bord*.

The anecdote is recounted to affirm that navigation is often a slightly imprecise science of small differences between practice and theory, and that there is often some discrepancy between what a precision instrument like a GPS is capable of giving and what the navigator at sea can 'get away with'. Perhaps this is why it is often referred to as the Art of Navigation, rather than the science.

The incident also illustrates why salesmen's tales of proven precision also need digesting with care and a pinch of the salt of reality. We also had one seller boasting that he had tied his boat alongside a quay and verified his exact position from a very large scale chart. He had then compared his own GPS with several other makes and was claiming greater accuracy and selection acumen for what he had purchased. The proof postulated was a comparison of the displayed positions expressed to 0.001 of a nautical mile. As we mentioned earlier, the third decimal figure equates to about six feet and even on the largest scale chart, a pencil line covers more than this. When we come down to distances of less than fifty metres in practical navigation, 'near enough' is generally good enough — but it does make you feel sorry for the customer services and complaints department of an equipment supplier.

Accuracy and Stability

If you really wish to see the effects of GPS accuracy and stability, about the best way is to interface a receiver with a chart plotter containing a map cartridge of generous scale — say 1:3,500 or even 1:12,500 — which makes one inch on the chart equal about 100 yards (90m). The chart plotter will have a trace, or track a history which draws a line showing where the boat has been. It achieves this by using an electronic line to join together the GPS derived positions taken at intervals selected by the operator.

If the boat is stationary, there should be no trace line. In practice, however, if you leave the GPS/plotter combination switched on for twelve hours at a fixed location, there will be a whole spider's web of track history woven inside that 200-metre diameter circle of uncertainty, which we have already discussed.

A poor quality receiver may have several points which pass well outside this 200-metre parameter, whereas a full multi-channel unit, well installed in a good location will have a very heavy concentration of trace lines at the centre of the circle (ie at the ship's position) with comparatively few very far away from it.

Track Accuracy

A track accuracy test run should be with the GPS (or better still GPS and plotter) in the car, which you then drive around a very regular square, rectangle or diamond-shaped route. This has, for instance, been done around a block of buildings, or by marking an area with something like 300 — 400-metre sides on an open space like an airfield or racecourse. A good map would probably even suggest some suitable quiet roads.

As you progress, watch the plotter position indicator. Does it turn when you turn? If you leave the track history running, do the corners coincide with each other on every circuit? Or do they continue beyond the corner, then cut back to rejoin the line showing the next 'leg'? (Fig 22)

Figure 22

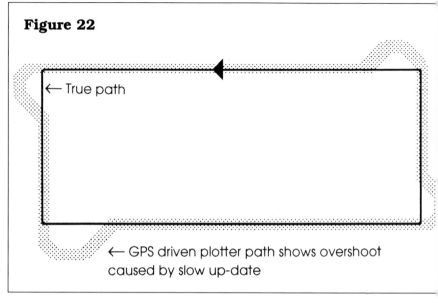

← True path

← GPS driven plotter path shows overshoot
caused by slow up-date

If the plotted shape is anything very different from
your actual route shape it indicates slow up-date and
poor averaging of fixes. I would expect our Model B from
Chapter Four to be in lock-step with you most of the
way.

Velocity Reliability

A velocity reliability test is very simple to effect. The
vehicle is driven on a straight line at a very steady speed
— 30 mph (or 35kph) are suitable. (You will probably
need to look at the Set-Up menu of your GPS receiver
and change the display to mph/kph, or you multiply
knots by 1.15 to do the conversion into mph.) Your GPS
derived speed should match your car speed both in rate
and in any change of rate. It should be very steady as
long as your speed is steady.

When you come to a stop, this should very quickly
show as zero on the screen. Then if you accelerate very
gently away again, the GPS display should exactly parallel your progress in rate and time.

Even though this is a very simple test, it is a very good one, because it will soon show up the two factors which decrease accuracy and reliability.

Many poorly screened and indifferently designed GPS receivers create a vast amount of interference noise. Every piece of wire is potentially a transmitting and receiving antenna, which can become an active radiator and receiver of electromagnetic energy just as soon as you excite it with a voltage. This 'white noise' is not of the type usable to boost signals — it is too steady and of the wrong sort. It just gets in the way and upsets the calculations.

Much of this noise can be generated by the internal clock. For good GPS efficiency, the clock must obviously be of the best, but some manufacturers who are 'building to a price' save money by using poor quality clocks.

Some receivers try to get over this shortcoming by averaging perhaps the last five readings and using this figure as present velocity. This can take anything up to ten seconds in extreme cases and your change in velocity from 30 mph to zero would step down over that period as the new averaging figures are taken in. Typically, it would go on halving (and showing these halves sequentially on the screen) until zero is reached.

In coarse terms, this is not catastrophic, but is a nuisance for somebody like a rally driver needing to travel at a precise speed, or a pilot required to maintain a steady speed for a required time for the legs of a holding pattern. On the boat, a good receiver which immediately and accurately reflects velocity change is very useful when you are sail trimming. If you are travelling at supersonic speed, small changes may not be important, but on our cruising boat plodding along at about five knots, a half knot increase is good news which would, for instance, give you six more miles on a twelve hour run, or get you into harbour about a hour earlier.

Dynamic Accuracy

This is another simple but interesting check on performance. As you drive past any marker — lamp post or signpost — activate the 'Position Store' button. If you then drive round to come back to this same spot, you should get a reading which is very close to your button push figure.

Here you are testing just how quickly the position is stored and whether it is accurate. It should show the same either when you stop at your marker again, or as you drive slowly past. A good receiver will be spot on, but your poorer model will show a discrepancy in time and distance, which might be very disconcerting on a power cruiser doing thirty-five knots and somebody goes over the side and you activate the GPS Man-Overboard switch.

Poor Location

The poor location tests are carried out by driving your GPS unit to where there are plenty of electrical cables and other lumps of metal and wire likely to reflect signals, distort them and put them out of phase. Poor performance means lack of quality engineering and filtering inside the antenna pod and in the black box itself. It might well persuade you that the unit under examination is not suitable for a fishing trawler, or any other commercial vessel.

Then try the unit out beneath some trees. If it is a damp autumnal day, so much the better. It is a peculiarity of microwaves that they are attracted to and are absorbed by water. Because of the way it grows, a tree's roots, trunk and foliage all have a high moisture content, even on a dry day and this can attenuate the signal enough to create errors.

(A further demonstration of this phenomenon is seen when you make a cup of soup in a microwave oven. The rays are attracted to the liquid and make it very hot but the cup remains quite cool.)

In navigational practice, a good GPS receiver is relatively impervious to moisture, but a poor one will go 'on the wobble' in hailstorms, or even when the boat is banging about in a seaway, throwing up spray and your GPS is being asked to lock on to a satellite quite close to the horizon.

Tests are interesting and enable you to learn your receiver's logic, displays and keyboard conventions, even if you live many miles from the sea. They extend your pleasure into the close season. Above all, they show the limitations never mentioned in the brochures and usually totally denied by the sales agent.

If this chapter has only taught you to read the fine print of equipment specifications quite carefully and to back up this perusal with some very sharp questions, it might save you from being disappointed in a purchase and should certainly prevent you from wasting money on equipment which does not do the thing you wish at the level you need for safety.

Chapter 6

GPS and Its Workmates

At its best, a sophisticated GPS unit is capable of being the engine room and the control unit to drive a large and increasing number of associated devices. It does this by collecting information, not only from the satellites, but also from a range of other systems such as wind direction and barometer and amalgamating all this data into formats which are very useful to the navigator.

It is now possible to use an installed GPS to take over total, unmanned control of a ship. We once sat in storm-bound Penzance en route for Scotland and joked that we had enough on-board technology to send the motor yacht, which we were delivering, round Land's End on its own. The crew could then have taken a hire car north to pick up the boat again somewhere off the Isle of Man.

At the time it was jokey talk, but underneath was the realisation that it could have been done with that particular vessel, thanks to the reliable position fixing of GPS, not only telling the ship where it is, but also directing it to turn away from radar recorded, unexpected objects. There are obvious dangers to this unmanned proposal, but it is not a piece of science fiction. By a combination of GPS, autopilot, chart plotter, radar and personal computer, the ship can run itself and even send data on everything being monitored back to a controlling shore station.

Because all these ancillary tools need to talk to each other, they need a common language spoken at an agreed speed. In the past, a number of electronics companies have used a combination of computer and graphics technologies, allied with expertise from telephone line modem and facsimile message methods, to let their instruments monitoring speed, depth, position etc talk to each other. The problem was that they could only talk to members of their own family. The commercial attraction to this limitation is that having been inveigled into buying one item from a particular supplier, you were forced into getting the remaining equipment from the same source. If they did not actually manufacture what you wanted, that was tough luck.

It has been largely through the powerful and universal acceptance of GPS and the realisation that it had such wide application, that manufacturers saw their own esoteric languages as limiting their sales, rather than enforcing customer loyalty. There was a sudden clamour for an international electronic language able to pass navigation and pilotage data between equipment, irrespective of source.

The solution was a GPS and data tongue under the banner of the National Maritime Electronics Association. There have been several improvements to the original NMEA protocol. We are currently on one of the versions of a language called NMEA 0183, (normally spoken of as NMEA one eight three) which is grandly described as 'an 8 bit ASCII, parity disabled, block orientated protocol for data transfer'.

ASCII is a computer language using binary codes standardised by the American Standard Code for Information Interchange.

A 'Protocol' in computer language means a set order in which information is passed so that the recipient device knows to what the figures relate.

In many ways, that neatly encapsulates the understanding of NMEA 0183. It is a series of phrases transmitted from a Talker, to any number of Listeners, in an agreed order, to make up a sentence. In dealing with the sort of information which a GPS-guided boat needs, it is useless to send the figure ten if the computers do not know whether this refers to boat speed, wind velocity or compass deviation.

In NMEA 0183, it knows perfectly unambiguously, because each morsel of information is contained in a phrase and each phrase is not only given a numbered place in a sentence, but the phrases are also always transmitted in the same order and each has a unique identification symbol at its start. The phrases are also separated from each other by commas and these are sent in the message even if there is no data between them. So by counting the commas and decoding the ident, a receiving Listener knows whether the incoming information refers to boat, or wind, or a destination. In addition to its own identifier, each sentence has a terminator — a back-up to all else to tell the Listener that a new information segment is about to begin. By this method, not only is data passed in general terms, but it can also have a particular address — eg sending a change of compass course to an autopilot, or giving a chart plotter information on a new route.

Once you begin to understand Neema One Eight Three, you begin to see what an incredibly versatile language it is and how much keyboard work and time can be saved by using it. The present software version can use about thirty-five different sentences, each transferring information about a different subject, varying from barometric pressure at sea level, via true or apparent wind force and direction, or satellite status, right on to time to reach next waypoint — with much more besides.

It also has a contribution to make to safety by decreasing the chance of accident caused by navigational error. In traditional navigation, many errors are due to mistakes in arithmetic. Many of us, for instance, are not adept at working to unusual arithmetic bases, so we find it difficult to add and subtract hours, minutes and seconds, or to multiply in degrees and minutes, so we make errors. Many GPS units have an in-built calculator to do this for you and also to handle the very large numbers which confuse many of us.

In electronic navigation, many accidents happen because a careless operator hit a wrong key, or transposed two figures whilst entering data. Most units will squeal if data is very incorrect but, in any event, as long as the operator has checked the information when it is put into the system, it will always be correctly passed from — say — GPS to autopilot or repeater, no matter how many times it is used.

This does not remove the need for traditional navigational skills. A poor navigator will be an indifferent pilot no matter how much electronic equipment you give him. Indeed much of this gear not only sharpens the navigator's abilities, but also makes him learn new ones. Some understanding of how NMEA 0183 works is undoubtedly one of these.

The Neema sentence passing a position in latitude and longitude is a good example of phrases making up a sentence and can be seen from the block explanatory paragraph and the ensuing extra explanation.

Figure 23

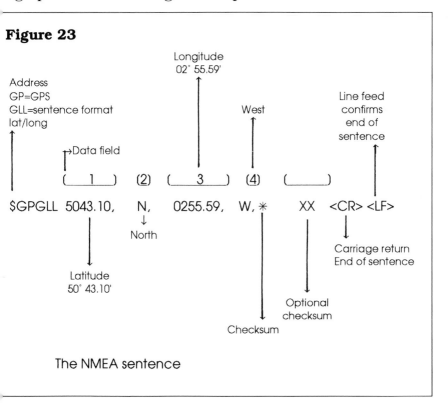

The NMEA sentence

$ THE DOLLAR SIGN is often used in computer language to denote the commencement of a new activity.

GP (GPS) is one of many abbreviations which are used in 'GPS speak'. They range from the esoteric WCV for Waypoint Closure Velocity to the commonly understood COG or Course Over Ground which will be familiar to anyone who has used Decca or other position-fixing electronics.

GLL is a sentence formatter which confirms which language is being spoken and which spacing conventions and symbols are to be employed.

DATA FIELD is a space between commas and carries actual navigational information, as opposed to other segments of the sentence which are giving instructions about how the sentence should be decoded.

LATITUDE AND LONGITUDE are normally passed in decimal notation of degrees, minutes and decimal fractions of a minute (base 100 or 1000) rather than degrees, minutes and seconds (base 60). It should be noted that many GPS receivers can calculate co-ordinates to three decimal places, or one thousandth of a nautical mile. This is of little value to the sea navigator, but has many applications in surveying. The on-board computers of a good GPS unit will rapidly convert base 60 readings to base 100, or vice versa.

CHECKSUM is a computer tool often used to verify that a computer disk's information is correct and is here put in to ensure that the data is as it should be, ie that a letter has not crept into a latitude field, which should only contain figures. It is always the last passive action agent of a Neema sentence and is usually followed by the active instructions.

<CR> <LF> carriage return and line feed which are familiar to computer users in their overlapping functions of starting a new line and telling the printer to move the paper (or screen) up the measured distance to accommodate it.

The sentence described is relatively simple in having only four data fields. The sentences giving the bearing to a selected Waypoint has twelve phrases in addition to its instructions and can even differentiate between those required for a Rhumb Line course, or for Great Circle navigation.

A simple GPS unit will offer the operator no control over the information to be passed, so its computer will scan over all the possibilities to see what is available. This makes it a bit slower and uses up memory which could have been made available for something more useful. A better (more expensive) unit will have separate ports for putting information in and sending it out — eg to download all Waypoint information to a computer so that it does not use up memory, then to put it all back in again when required. In action, the operator is offered the choice of what data is to be passed around, eg — fuel flow, apparent wind, autopilot instructions and so on. By not hunting for information which is not required, the computer becomes faster and can turn its energies to other functions.

Which GPS Assisted Tools and Why

Once you have a sophisticated GPS unit in situ, you have a power house of energy and a wide spectrum of possible things it can cause to happen because of its very rapid up-date of position, its accurate time-keeping and its computer's ability to calculate distances, angles and times. In order to do this, the GPS central processing unit needs additional information from such devices as the fluxgate compass controlling the autopilot. To get this — and to pass out data and instructions — it needs to be connected or inter-faced to them. (In navigational practice the two terms are synonymous.)

The Autopilot

This is generally the first unit that a GPS beginner considers suitable for GPS connection and control. Even though I have used autopilots for many years, I am still fascinated by the way it constantly alters the ship's head to maintain the compass course which has been set.

Navigators soon come to terms with fundamental limitation, that even when the bows are constantly pointing West, the lateral effects of wind and tide might mean that the boat is slipping diagonally left and really travelling nearer to South-West. This is the difference between Course and Course Over the Ground (COG) or Course Made Good (CMG) which is simply called Track (TRK) by some manufacturers.

(This last point needs treating with a bit of care. To some software writers it equates to COG or CMG, but others use it to denote the heading of a straight line drawn between two Waypoints on a chart.)

When the autopilot is interfaced with a GPS unit, the one second up-date of new position is converted into a new course to steer to the next WP. If the boat is being moved sideways, the autopilot receives instructions to nudge the head back round towards the target. There are obvious advantages here, say, when a ship is constantly having its head knocked sideways by big waves, or strong gusts of wind. It will steam on the diagonal course until the autopilot manages to regain control and to return the head to the original course set. The vessel will move forward in a series of zigzags and if allowed to continue uncorrected will end up some distance off to the side of its destination.

Although a GPS interfaced autopilot will overcome this problem and is a very sophisticated pilotage tool for a power boat in still water, an honest, practical navigator will see its limitations elsewhere. On our own motor-sailer, for example, when a tide is slicing diagonally into the bow, it obviously slows the boat down, so we make much better progress over the ground by just letting the boat go sideways. If the autopilot was constantly turning the bows back directly into a two knot tide, our speed would be slowed by this amount. That would be using GPS and autopilot combination very badly.

Even though we have the interface in situ, the only time we are able to let GPS drive the boat is when there is no tide and the wind is on the quarter. Then the autopilot GPS combination makes boat handling a real idle pleasure.

The Chart Plotter

On its own, this is a relatively low priority device, which puts a miniaturised marine chart up onto a VDU screen and adds waypoints, routes and other navigational information by means of a keyboard and a cursor usually controlled by a tracker ball. As a stand-alone instrument it is a useful planning tool but that is about all. However, once the chart plotter is interfaced with a GPS receiver, it becomes so incredibly versatile that it totally alters the way in which most of us drive our boats.

The interface is very swiftly accomplished by a couple of wires and puts onto the screen a small, flashing cursor showing the boat's position at the present time. (This is displayed as the graphic and as lat/long at the screen edge.) As the boat moves, so the displayed position changes and this shift can be drawn in as a fine line indicating the boat's direction of travel and the distance covered — sometimes called 'trace, or 'track', or 'track history'. Once you have these two factors (ie actual position, position X minutes ago) a phenomenal amount of navigational data can be extrapolated from it. This adds many more applications to the chart plotter.

We shall talk about this in more detail when we discuss GPS in an actual cruise plan but, as an aperitif, just think of the advantages of an electronic line pivoted on the boat's position. If you wish to know your distance off a half-tide rock marked on the screened chart, you put the cursor on the hazard, press a button and get accurate information about heading and distance from you. You can do the same with buoys which only show on the radar as blobs, but you can get their distance and heading from the boat by using this combination of GPS position and plotter graphics. Our magic

Two examples of chart plotters from Philips. This equipment becomes an extremely useful navigational tool when linked to a GPS system.

electronic line only needs to be stretched out to the same figures and the buoy beneath the cursor is verified as the one on the screen. Another button push will display a screen edge info box with details of the identity and characteristics of the object in question.

Yacht Racing

Yacht race control also uses GPS, which can be interfaced to a transmitting device and will send details of each competitor's current position back to the race control point, where it is displayed on a screen overlaid with a chart of the race area. The screen can show a number of yachts at the same time, so the organisers of events like races around the world, always know where each boat is at any given time. A canny skipper would also have the gizmo on his boat to keep track of the opposition.

Repeaters
These are part and parcel of cruising boats, on which a good format is to have the main GPS unit snug and dry down in the nav station and a waterproof repeater giving pilotage essentials out near the tiller or on the flybridge.

Data Back-up
A data back-up facility is useful both in cruising terms and for such people as commercial fishermen. There are a couple of GPS units around with a transmission port to store Waypoint information on an ordinary portable tape recorder, via a link to its microphone socket. This device works well enough, but there are even more exciting possibilities for storing GPS derived positions on a computer diskette, or of passing data from the diskette, to be loaded into a GPS unit, which will then find its way from the present position to whichever of them you choose.

A spin-off from this is to sit at a home computer screen to plan your route and to work out courses, distances and co-ordinates, then to take the diskette to the boat in order to up-load your data so that the GPS unit can process the information and use it to give you directions.

Safety
A Radio safety aid already exists as a small black box which sits in tandem with a VHF microphone and will send out a repeated spoken Mayday signal not only giving your boat's name and the number of persons on board, but also the very latest position passed to it from the GPS unit.

All these navigation aids are but the tip of an exciting electronic and GPS iceberg which grows bigger, wider and more interesting with every day that passes.

Chapter 7

Installation

How and where you install your GPS navigator is important in a number of respects. If the magic box is
mounted where you can see it easily and reach it
comfortably, then you are likely to use it more often. This
extra use makes you more familiar with the logic of the
keyboard and, therefore, less likely to make mistakes
when you have to do things in a hurry. You become a
safer seaman because of this expertise

It also seems a pity that a person can pay the relatively
big money needed to buy a GPS, then not get the
maximum enjoyment from it because the installation is
poor.

The mounting of the antenna as opposed to the display
usually offers less choice of site, but still needs care.

One of the better aspects of GPS technology is that the
actual physical and electrical installation is very simple
and generally self protected against reverse polarity and
the other voltage 'faux pas' which amateurs are inclined
to make. The work should be well within the competence
of any boat owner and usually will not merit the attention of an electronics engineer, whose bill for labour and
— in some cases — the high fee demanded for permission to go into a marina, can come to almost 50% of the
cost of the receiver itself.

Most GPS rigs need no more than a voltage supply, and
two connectors for the signal line and braid of the
antenna. (Some might need an earth, but this is only a
single wire to an anode, or to any other straight passage
to ground). If you are interfacing with other instruments,
a simple set-up needs only two wires and even a full
input/output system can get away with four connections.

This simplicity is not a writer's exaggeration. Indeed,
one of our own GPS units arrived with a screwdriver, a

hex key, a few screws, a couple of cable ties and a very slender, four-page installation manual. We only needed to add cable strippers and a knife to the tool chest — and this because we were shortening the cables for our own convenience. The whole installation operation took just under an hour from opening the box to switching on a fully earthed GPS, interfaced to the chart plotter and also sending its NMEA signals to the radar — if required.

When you begin to make your sketches and draw up an installation plan (which you are certainly going to keep with the ship's papers) there are four main factors to consider. They are:
1 The display
2 The antenna
3 The power supply
4 The earth

The Display

The display and where to put it probably gives most of us the biggest headache. We certainly dither and argue about this more than just about any other task on board. Again there are a number of important parameters to observe.

Legibility

This is obviously one of the first things to consider when you are discussing mounting sites. You must be able to see the screen and to read all the digits without error and without performing cranial gymnastics. You need to be able to do this from where you normally work, ie sitting at a chart table, or from where you normally steer the boat.

Good GPS units have excellent displays which remain very legible from a wide variety of angles, but some of the smaller, less contrasty LCD screens need siting with extreme care. Anybody who owned an early digital watch will understand this and also realise that the ambient light is also important.

Some LCD screens have so little low light contrast that eye strain is almost inevitable, whilst others have the same reaction to bright sunlight. In the old days, the screen of many instruments used to go temporarily black if exposed to bright sunlight. In fact, it is heat rather than light, which causes the discolouration, but there are now screens with a high degree of in-built protection against this malady. It pays to ask your dealer before you sign the cheque.

A spin-off advantage to a GPS unit with an integral simulator is, not only does it enable you to learn all the functions at home, but if the simulator is run during installation, it lets you pick the optimum site (and angle if you are setting the box into a console) for comfortable viewing of all the display screens, with no need to connect-in an antenna to get some pictures. In this way you can verify that you do not lose the digits in the corner of the screen for certain menu pages and can try numerous options of tilt for better LCD contrast.

Visibility

An interesting idea to play with. Most small yachts have a chart table at the foot of the companionway, but are driven from the cockpit. If the skipper requires continuous information, and does not buy a cockpit repeater, he must install his GPS unit so that he can see it and read it from both stations. A number of colleagues have accomplished this by installing the display at the table, but so that it can be seen from the cockpit door. An alternative is to mount the display on a swivelling board which can be turned out-wards in the shelter of the doorway for viewing by cockpit crew, or hinged back and in for use at the navigation table.

Reach

A factor which came late to my thinking. We currently have two GPS units on the boat. One is on a ledge forward of the wheel and beyond our wheelhouse sloping chart table. It can only be reached by leaning across the steering wheel with constant risk that the autopilot gives the rudder a twitch and a spoke either hits the navigator in the solar plexus, or catches in his clothing and drags him off balance.

The other unit is mounted just above head height on the wheelhouse after bulkhead. To use the keyboard, you have to reach up. To put in even a short list of nine way-points, you need to make about twenty-five keystrokes per position, which is not only tiring on the arm, but also gives a crick in the neck. If the boat is underway and the navigator needs one hand to support himself in waves, he cannot hold his notes where he can see them all the time and in-put errors become almost inevitable.

When you are contemplating where to put your display, just remember that you will spend lots of time pushing buttons, so you need to be able to reach them quickly, easily and safely.

Protection

Protection from the elements needs clarification and confirmation by the chandler, especially if your unit is to be installed outside — even under the shelter of a cuddy, or a spray hood. There is a huge difference in terminology and meaning between, splash-proof, water-resistant, water-protected and totally waterproof. This latter should be taken to mean that the case can be totally immersed in water to a depth of about five metres with no fear of incursion, or of corrosion of terminals and connectors.

Because many GPS products come from America, the totally environmentally safe GPS should have passed the standard test leading to US Coast Guard spec CFR 46, in which gallons of pressurised water are directed at the product for a period of several minutes without the tiniest drop getting inside and with no diminution of instrument performance.

Theft

Protection from thieves is altogether a different sort of problem. The best solution is to install your GPS in such a manner that it can be removed and hidden when you will be absent for a short period, or removed and taken home with you when the boat is left on the moorings for any length of time.

Open Boats

Small open boats need special installation considera-
tions. Obviously only the totally waterproof survive. Our
best solution to date has been to mount our dive RIB's
electronics on a lift-off box attached to the steering
console by bolts and easy-to-operate thumb-screw nuts.
The box contains GPS, VHF radio, echo sounder and a
fluxgate compass display. All the connections are via
waterproof sockets on the box and plugs on the connecting leads. Inside the box, there is a distribution box to
send the electric power to the several instruments,
together with connection plugs and distributors for the
video echo sounder and fluxgate heading sensor. It is a
total boat control station in miniature.

The Mark Two version of the removable box will also
have a permanently mounted, jelly-filled 12v motorcycle
battery with a split relay charger — also fed in via a
waterproof plug. Such a device could charge from boat,
car or any other suitable recharging mechanism. This
could run all the electronics, either as a stand-by, or
even all the time. It would also enable you to program
the GPS at home before a trip and with no need to find
an external low voltage power source.

Antenna

The GPS antenna comes in many shapes, sizes and
formats. We have already discussed the possible effects
of installation position on performance, but it bears
repeating that antenna height above sea level is not a
consideration. All things being equal, a GPS antenna
mounted at deck level will perform as well as one
mounted on the flybridge and probably better than one
put at the top of a swaying fifty-foot mast.

Installation criteria should be more geared to giving the
aerial a totally unobstructed circular view of the horizon
and of the sky seen as a dome shape above the antenna tip,
from a place where it is not likely to get clouted by sheets,
blocks and staggering crew members, nor used as a handle
to help uninitiated visitors up the boarding ladder.

Almost all GPS antennae feeders are of low loss co-axial cable which is sufficiently well screened to be wound in a tight coil to tuck away the excess, without such proximity and loop effect degrading the signal. Most aerials come with sufficient cable to reach from mast-head to navigation table. If you plan to shorten the co-axial, do not forget to check with the supplier that this feeder is not part of the electrical (or resonant) length of the receiving unit. It also pays to verify that shortening the antenna cable will not be construed as modifying the equipment and invalidating the warranty.

Power Supply

This should not be a problem of quantity. There are people who look at our all-electric and all-electronic boat management set-up, then suck their teeth, shake their heads and comment on battery drain. It is wasted emotion because a typical big GPS receiver is rated at seven Watts maximum, which means that it is only pulling 0.58 amps (amps = Watts divided by volts) which would let a standard seventy amp-hour marine battery run the unit for at least four days without recharge.

This position is enhanced because many receivers go into 'sleep mode', drawing just a few milliamps if no keys are operated for a period which can either be factory set at something like five minutes, or user programmed. During this repose, the machine continues to track the satellites and to up-date such data as position, course and speed, but this is not displayed. It is the screen and its back-lighting which are the most current hungry.

Voltage spikes and other surges can be a problem. If, for example, your boat is on a single battery and this is also feeding an autopilot, a fridge, an automatic bilge pump and the electronics, these coming on together can cause a sudden huge demand which will cause the GPS to sound an alarm and even to switch off. This is not usually harmful to the equipment because most of the better quality gear has a diode network protective against reversed polarity and power surges.

The problem is more prevalent on boats using outboard motors, some of which have an unregulated voltage output. We have, for instance, measured over twenty volts coming from a very large two-stroke outboard motor immediately after a cold start, when the batteries were demanding a high rate of recharge. This 'spike' does no good at all to a piece of electronic apparatus whose specification quotes '12 volt battery, but range not to exceed 15 Vdc'.

It always pays to read the technical spec. In much purpose-built marine gear, the specification and safety parameters are very high with automatic sensing 12 or 24 volts usable without switching and giving a 10.5 — 32 Vdc tolerance. However, in spite of this tolerance, we always shut down all our electronics both when we are starting the dive boat's big outboard, or flashing up the fifty-horse diesel on the motor-sailer. We do this even when the engine is warm and starting so brief that the displays only flicker. Call it pessimism, or belt and braces, or any other name, but it makes us feel safer and puts our instruments to less risk.

For open boats (and as a back-up on larger craft) a 12 volt portable power pack is a useful item to have on your Christmas and birthday present shopping list. We have one which is rechargeable from either the car cigarette lighter socket, or from the ship's supply. It is rated to four Ampere hours and would run the electronics for long enough for us to sort out any problem. It also has a hundred other uses around the boat including a 12v soldering iron and a portable searchlight. For an open boat it could be an ideal power supply solution in its own right.

Integral batteries are usually the power source for hand-held and portable GPS models. In our own experience, they are generally not good news. For many seasons, we have employed such power supplies for hand-held radios at sea and notebook computers ashore. When they arrive at the quoted time that a machine will run on its own battery, the manufacturers must be using the equipment very differently from our own modus operandi. We generally divide the quoted time by two and still keep our fingers crossed. Unfortunately, many GPS receivers also follow this malady.

There are two possible solutions to this irritant.

Firstly, if you are best served by a hand portable GPS unit, opt for one with a slide-on Nicad battery and purchase a spare. Secondly, look at the models which are also usable (and often rechargeable) from a normal 12v battery, so that whenever possible your power is from the ship or vehicle supply. It really does make for safety and sense to pay a bit extra for one of these dual supply and charge source units.

Data Transfer

This also influences installation because of the two most common systems in use and also because some manufacturers still retail equipment using an esoteric interface language — generally their own — for reasons already discussed.

We have also already discussed the sense of being able to pass data from one instrument and site to another. Possibly the most common is to have a GPS display at the helm position and to install a chart plotter, or a multifunction display down in the comfort of the navigation area.

There are two ways of achieving this information sharing. Some manufacturers, for example, use a — so-called — black box, central collection unit, which gathers up and processes into NMEA 0183 protocol all the essential, raw information. Separate sensor cables bring in information about depth, boat speed, wind characteristics and — of course — GPS derived data referring to position, bearing to destination and time. Once the separate items have been translated into 0183, they are passed via a single cable link to the first instrument in the chain. There, the relevant facts are taken out and the remainder passed along to the next display, where the process is repeated.

There are a number of advantages to this method.

1 The most sensitive items — like EPROMs etc — are in a strong box in a sheltered place.

2 Once the box has been sited, the installation cable route difficulties are minimal.

3 If a malfunction or other problem occurs, the central unit is a good place to begin your troubleshooting, which can often be diagnosed/rectified by lifting out one plug-in module and trying a replacement.

4 The black box can be equipped with an electronic translation device allowing you to mix and match different protocol and data transfer languages.

The disadvantage is that the loss of one instrument could cause them all to fail, especially if this is down to a blown fuse: however, most have an unbreakable by-pass path, keeping the remaining displays alive if one part of the chain fails. If you link together a long chain of displays and their power supply is all on the data cable, there is inevitably some voltage drop towards the end of the line. This can only be remedied by inserting a second power supply line into the system, but this can be a bit messy and even complicate an installation which was meant to be simple.

The alternative method is to connect the separate sensors, antennae and transducers directly to the instrument displays which they are designed to feed, then to 'daisy chain' the instruments together with a cable which absorbs data as it passes along the chain.

In this way, the GPS data is travelling down to a repeater via — for example — the compass which is adding information about magnetic deviation and variation which, in turn, affects the instructions given to the autopilot to steer a course to the next waypoint as calculated by the GPS number cruncher.

The advantages of separates are:

1 They are separate and autonomous, so losing one display to a breakdown does not mean that you lose the lot.

2 It is very simple to feed power to each separate unit (or to pass it via the link cable) and to have them individually switched. Then, if you are at anchor and just want to check on the wind strength, you are only switching on the relevant device, rather than the whole chain. Similarly, you can power up the GPS in order to put in tomorrow's waypoints, without lighting up the twelve back-lit displays in your chain and watching the battery charge level go into rapid decline.

3 If one instrument breaks down, the location of the fault is in simple isolation.

The disadvantage of separates is also simply that they are separate, which can make the routing of cables rather more complex and needing more wire.

In all fairness, there is not much to choose between the two methods. Both have their aficionados and both are plagued by antagonists. There is very little difference in cost, so most of us end up by buying what appeals to us in the safe knowledge that choice is a matter of opinion, but that practicality and functionality are matters of fact. Both systems work and work well.

For most leisure users, there is as much pleasure in buying and installing products which appeal to you as there is in actually using them. For both amateurs and professionals alike, if the instrumentation is attractive, simple to use and well installed, you are more likely to use it more often and that makes you a safer and more efficient operator.

Chapter 8

A GPS Passage

The clubhouse Luddites who claim to be able to thread a fifty-foot yacht through the eye of an unknown needle with no more navaids than a wetted finger to test the wind, persistently mock GPS and its users. Their arguments are that they have always managed without electronic aids and fear that their adoption leads to an erosion of their traditional navigational skills. They frequently ask what the skipper will do if an electronic instrument breaks down.

Such arguments are relatively easy to counter. In the first place, properly installed and tested electronic equipment is strongly built and very reliable. There is no reason to fear that it will break down any more than we now expect our digital clocks and watches to fail. In the very unlikely event of mechanical failure which cannot be repaired by replacing a fuse, or some other immediate, on-board solution, we do as we always did — for example, on a long passage during which a careless sailor knocked the ship's sextant off a bench and the impact put the mirror out of alignment. We cope. We fall back on the ship's log notes of course and speed and revert to dead reckoning and estimated positions as we have always done.

Whereas few small ships have a second, bulky sextant available, our own boat has twin GPS units on separate circuits and we also carry a rechargeable 12 volt power pack which would run a GPS unit for a couple of days. At the end of this time, if we had not managed to restore the ship's power, we could fire up the generator and run the systems from that.

In real extremis, we can back up electronics with electronics and use the radio direction finder, which is still waiting in the wings for such an emergency. We have not had to employ it in real earnest for several years now, but in the pre-electronic days often needed it to back up a slightly suspect sextant position — especially when closing a strange coastline and wanting to feel more comfortable with more position precision.

It also has to be admitted (even by the Luddites) that you can often go for several days without seeing the noonday sun, or being able to get a sextant site on a star. We have certainly had such total cloud cover on a couple of straight line Biscay passages. Then, the sextant was totally useless, but the electronic navigation systems just went on up-dating every single second of every day. As we neared the (cloudy and misty) north-west tip of Spain it was very comforting to know our position to within 100 metres or so.

Equally, in spite of modern trans-national co-operation, news of changed buoys and alterations to lights and light-house sequences are not always immediately passed to other maritime authorities and even then the correction can take several months to appear in print. There are few sensations worse than sailing in towards the land, but finding that none of the lighthouses are flashing with the characteristics shown in your pilot books. In harbour entrances, where you might run aground, the feelings of anxiety are even worse when what you can see does not match up with what the chart tells you to expect.

It is then that you are thankful for your investment in a good GPS receiver. If you can use it well, you always know exactly where you are and it only requires a little chartwork to tell you where to steer to reach your destination safely.

We should constantly remind ourselves that a GPS navi-gator is a combination of a radio frequency receiver and a small computer, so it suffers all the blessings and shortcom-ings of the latter — especially the GIGO syndrome. Garbage In means Garbage Out. In this sense, GPS does not remove the need for traditional navigational skills. Properly and safely used, GPS is not a substitute for the navigation officer's black arts with paper, pencil, charts and mental arithmetic, but an addition to them. It is a safer addition, because whereas most people's arithmetic and trigonom-etry can be fallible, the computer's calculation powers are very rapid and — provided that you push the correct buttons — never wrong.

To see this marriage of traditional skills and modern hi-tech in true perspective, join us on a couple of legs of an annual pilgrimage which we make from the South Coast of England, around the west corner of France and across the top of Biscay to Bordeaux and the start of the Canal du Midi.

It is an interesting passage because it takes in a long, open sea crossing which flirts with the shipping lanes, then wriggles its way down the fast tides and tugging buoys of the inspiring Chenal du Four towards the notorious Raz de Sein. The journey cannot be accomplished without spending at least one complete night out at sea.

It is also always interesting to see how other navigators work (we all do things differently and can learn from each other) and how they run their boats. In this case it is a 28ft 6in (8.5m) Colvic Watson motor-sailer ketch, with a 50 hp diesel engine and a good range of instruments and systems. The boat can be autopilot driven from the wheelhouse, which is also the navigation area. Our aim is to try for a steady speed of round about five knots, but we are satisfied if we can make a hundred miles a day by using our two propulsion systems, either separately or in tandem — whichever is the most comfortable, efficient and economic.

The voyage actually starts a long time before it begins. We have the GPS at home, but can also use the chart plotter as a rough planning aid.

The approximate distances for each leg of the voyage, or for each route within a leg are always worked out from the plotter, for the simple reason that it can be done on one electronic chart, rather than having several charts, rulers and dividers scattered over the floor. Electronic distance information is a mere two button push task. These distances are used to calculate our running time at five knots or less, so they present the skipper in "What if?" mode, of working out what a speed decrease of 0.5 knots will do to the passage time.

The author's 28-foot motor-sailer

This factor is important on this particular voyage because we need to arrive at the top corner of Brittany exactly at high water Brest, in order to have the fast current with us and to carry one tide cycle down to the Raz de Sein, which is advisably taken at low water slack. If we get the timing wrong, we could have a very rough passage, or we might get twelve hours hanging around at a corner infested with cargo ships and fishing trawlers whilst waiting for the next ebb.

The plotter shows the distance from our home port to Portsall at the corner of Brittany to be 140 miles. We can do this in twenty-eight hours at five knots, but will leave a bit of spare time and assume that we can make four and a half knots and get a passage time of thirty-one hours, even if we have to put on a bit more coal to get better speed over the last three to four hours. On this occasion, we have a 17.00 HW Brest, so our departure needs to be at about 10.00 the day before. We are a drying harbour, which means that the next task is to look at the tide tables, in order to check our exit feasibility, or to decide whether we even need to make a much earlier start.

It seems that we can get away when we wish, so we will probably opt for a leisurely 08.00 — 08.30 departure.

Our plan, if the wind permits, is to put the boat on 210°T and take the Channel in a straight diagonal line.

Some navigators throw up their hands in horror when it is suggested that they should draw lines on their expensive charts. Safety-conscious professionals never do it any other way. Without the pencil line immediately to capture your eye, you spend a long time scanning before you have found your course projection. Additionally, the pencil line is a good check that you have not laid your course where it passes over rocks and shallows.

Here it will be appropriate to comment on the weakness of present day electronic navigation. Chart plotter displays are too small and too cluttered to show all the necessary information at the same time. For clarity, it is usually necessary to remove depth contours, or navigation marks from the screen which, at best, can lead to poor planning and can, at worst, be dangerous.

It is elementary — but very true — that GPS can only work in straight lines, which points a finger of doubt at those people who skimp on charts just because they have it on board. The machine will only give you the rhumb line course from A to B. If there is a shallow wreck or a half-tide rock along the way . . .

Along this trans Channel line, we mark off waypoints every twenty miles. These are always taken, with ruler and dividers, from the paper chart because its scale is large enough to get accuracy, which is not the case when you slide a cursor over an electronic screen.

These waypoints are next entered into the GPS unit as a specific route. It is here that the double checking and marriage of old and new begins. When I scan through the point-to-point distances and bearings, I should get a succession of 210°T and 20 Nm answers. The maximum acceptable discrepancy is 1 Nm and 2°. Very often there is a major difference on one leg, so we need to check all the co-ordinates. Mostly, the fault is not in the paper-work, but arises from pushing a wrong digital key on entry. Sometimes the key is correct, but is badly pushed, so the figure does not record and all subsequent entries are one space out of kilter.

With this part of the journey satisfactorily planned, we record all the waypoints in our record book. Occasionally, I also put them on a computer disk, or run the route through PC Wayplanner, which lets me look at how the boat will be slowed, pushed sideways, or even speeded up by the currents. This computer program also has the facility to take the waypoints down from our principal GPS, which drives the chart plotter and to feed them to its memory bank and even to pass them along to our secondary, smaller stand-by GPS. This is the lazy navigator's way of saving the labour of three separate, lengthy, keyboard sessions or, put another way, is using modern electronic communications at their best.

Actually on passage, I usually work out the ten-mile-apart, in-between waypoints for the crossing. These are just put in as dots on the paper chart and should take about two hours to travel, which coincides nicely with the times when we write up the log and with our two-handed crew's watch-keeping scheme of two hours on and two hours off. It is also a safe-guard against electric or electronic mishap, because we have a recent check on an accurate position and can begin our purely manual navigation from a known datum point.

We now have to turn our attention to the exciting passage down Le Chenal de Four, with the prospect of the overfalls and whirlpools and seven knot ebb at Le Raz de Sein — about six hours run and just right for one tide. The buoys and marks come in for the same treatment, ie we take the co-ordinates from the paper chart, work out the courses, distances and probable running times between them, transfer the data to the electronic systems by the easiest method and record the data into one of our permanent records.

Even though our ultimate stop-over destination will be Audierne, or one of the other South Brittany ports, we take the precaution of working out the best route into a diversion port. This is not a particularly friendly coast and we have occasionally needed to run into L'Abervrach, Le Conquet or Camaret because of poor weather, crew fatigue, or a boat problem. If we already have the turning points and safe marks recorded, we can later decide on when will be the best time to leave our route and dive for shelter.

All this navigational preparation and pre-programming of the GPS units takes but an evening to execute. It is an evening of sheer pleasure almost like doing an armchair cruise in its own right. It extends what is mostly a summer pastime into the winter.

Once we are ready for sea, the GPS begins to work quite hard for the cash it cost us. To protect this investment, we do not actually turn it on until the engine has been started and the battery charging settled to a level devoid of voltage spikes. Most equipment has a good deal of voltage surge and drain protection built in, but we are belt and braces people when it comes to going to sea.

Once we have illumination, we immediately turn up a screen which shows information about the health of the probable satellites and their direction from the boat and their angle above the horizon. With a bit of experience, you soon get to forecast if the GPS will lock on immediately, or whether it might need a bit of time. If it seems slow, we have a look at the HDOP screen.

Because our main unit drives a chart plotter, it can be sited where you can see one or the other from wherever you sit in the pilothouse. The plotter has a graphic representation of the chart, the route, the waypoints and the ship's position. This information is also digitally displayed, but the figures are rather small for reading from a distance.

This sort of information is better gleaned from our large screen GPS receiver. We normally set this to show in large letters and figures the navigation data which we consider to be most important to us. Probably our most used display screen is the one which has a large, clear digital display of (1) Bearing to waypoint (2) Distance to waypoint (3) Course over ground (4) Speed over ground (5) Amount of cross track error in nautical miles and decimal fractions. (Fig 25)

Figure 25

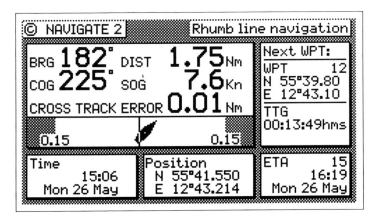

A selection of sub screens shows (1) The name and memory catalogue sequential number of the next way-point (2) The time to go to reach it and the waypoint closing velocity. This last is useful when you are beating to windward or being forced into a slanting course by the tide. It gives you an idea of how much progress you are making towards your destination and serves as a good decision making aid about where to tack, or when to put the boat's nose into the tide and fight your way through it.

This same screen also has a graphic display of the boat's position in relation to the rhumb line and a reminder of how wide you have set your off-course limits before the icon vanishes off the screen and an audio alarm sounds.

For the cross Channel passage of 140 miles, we set these limits at five miles, but will often be well outside them if we have a strong sideways tide. For the Chenal du Four, we set the limit lines at 0.25 miles, which is the maximum error which we allow ourselves.

The display is finished off with two small screens showing the Time to Go before we reach the last way-point in our route, plus the current time in minutes and seconds UT. We always leave all our navigation clocks in Universal Time (GMT) because that is what the satellites work in and to avoid the confusion and mental arith-metic of BST and French daylight-saving time and other time zones.

This particular journey of two separately stored routes has a number of interesting extra GPS features.

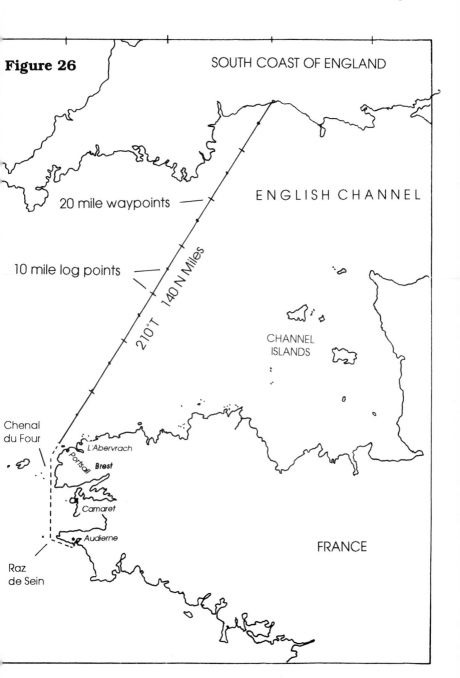

Figure 26

SOUTH COAST OF ENGLAND

ENGLISH CHANNEL

20 mile waypoints

10 mile log points

210°T 140 N Miles

CHANNEL
ISLANDS

Chenal
du Four

L'Abervrach

Portsall   **Brest**

Camaret

Audierne

FRANCE

Raz
de Sein

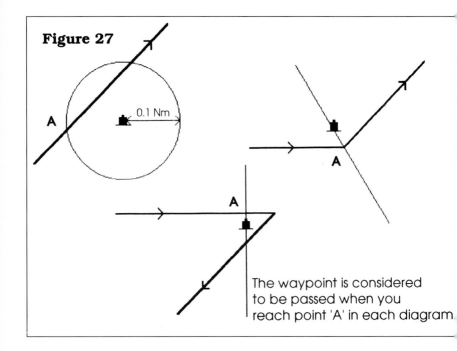

Figure 27

0.1 Nm

A

A

A

The waypoint is considered
to be passed when you
reach point 'A' in each diagram

The GPS can have several different methods of decid-
ing when it has passed a waypoint and is going onto the
next. A perfectly steered straight line is not a problem.
The audio indicator sounds as you actually pass
through the point. If, however, you have been pushed to
one side of your line, a different set of criteria arises and
this changes again if there is a change of course at the
waypoint involved. A prudent navigator changes the
waypoint pass criteria according to the straight lines
and angles the passage plan involves. The illustration
shows this more succinctly than any explanation in
words.

The chart for the Channel crossing is an Admiralty
derived version written to a OSGB 36 datum format,
so we need to check before departure that this is the
format being used by the GPS. Once we are beyond
the Portsall buoy at the top corner of Brittany, we are

on a much larger scale chart of the Chenal de Four based on information provided by the French Hydrographic Service and written to European Datum. The positional difference between them is only about 150 metres, but we may as well set the GPS datum point library to the correct one. The removal of absolutely any known source of potential imprecision is worth doing.

Being at sea is very little different from any other sphere of human endeavour in that successful execution is seventy five per cent dependent on careful preparation. With the GPS units properly programmed with data, their reliability and total disregard of atmospheric effects makes the seafarer feel very confident about where he is and where he is going. This, in turn, frees him from the slavery of extra hours at the chart table and slide rule and releases his eyes and brain to keep a sharp look-out and to manage the boat.

On our last helter-skelter zig-zag down the Chenal de Four, it was fascinating to watch Pakman (the nickname we have given to the flashing chart plotter cursor) showing the boat's GPS derived position, tracing our course from buoy to buoy. When the GPS told us that the twin towers of Les Platresses were 2.1 miles ahead, it was a marvellous feeling to open out the radar VRM to that distance and to observe its line cutting across two clear targets with a gap between them. As the tide got hold of the boat, the increase in speed showed on the GPS screen with much more accuracy than the paddle wheel log is able to give. Similarly, when we eased main, mizzen and genoa sheets as we turned away from the North-East wind, the extra knot of pace was immediately displayed and assisted us with the best sail settings.

At each of the turn points in this channel, the alarm sounded and we tweaked the autopilot onto the new course shown by the GPS and checked against our notes on the chart and the entries in the passage log.

For a navigator, there are few moments more frightening than being in fast tides near a dangerous coast and not knowing exactly where you are. The super attraction of GPS and its reliability and other attributes, is that as long as you have the chart, it should always be possible to plot your position with some precision and to know what is under the keel, no matter where on Earth you happen to be.

That alone makes GPS well worth having.

Is it worth making the switch to GPS?
A System Switch Box from Philips Navigation AS
allows you a choice of either Decca or GPS.

Chapter 9

GPS – The Last Word

Let us leave *The Yachtsman's GPS Handbook* via that same door which brought us into this amazing house of navigational progress, but let us also be very honest in our analysis of what we might have learned from the visit. It is undeniable that the act of making GPS available to the general public was certainly one of the greatest, forward navigation progress steps of this century. Being able to measure distance to accuracies of a few metres because of radio transmitters, clocks and computers, travelling at huge speed, over 11,000 miles in space, still totally fascinates me and I am excited that we are as yet only using about thirty per cent of the system's full potential.

Equally, as users, we need to keep a sense of perspective. GPS is a phenomenal navigational asset, but as a seagoing tool it will be many years before it comes anywhere near its theoretic levels of precision, or achieves the level of use which early protagonists tried to lead us to believe would have been reached by this point in time. We also need to take with a large pinch of salt some of the eulogies declaimed by salesmen, whose prime aim is to sell equipment.

The flooding of the market with hand-held GPS receivers is a case in point. The biggest profits will undoubtedly come from the land use of GPS for car tourers, walkers, public services, electronic mapping, haulage trade etc. The basic user technology for this is already well developed, but such back-up systems as local Differential GPS stations, GPS maps and overlays is nowhere near ready. Meanwhile, the marketing people are stuck with an attractive concept, which they are pushing at boat owners.

Let us be quite straight about this. In my own opinion,

a purely hand-held navigational system has absolutely no prime place on a serious seagoing vessel. All marine experience dictates that once you go out in waves, anything not bolted down will fall off a ledge, slide about the chart table, or get wet. At other times, it will get sat upon, be left at home, be crushed in a ditty bag, or will disappear into the pocket of a non-rightful owner. There is also the point that an advertised six-hour battery rarely lasts more than four in practice. These tiny devices can boast some fascinating electronics, but many of their functions are very difficult to use at sea. The very thought of trying to navigate a boat by using a 'plotter' screen just a couple of inches wide and made up of a handful of notchy pixels would be laughable where it not that people are actually persuaded into buying these gadgets for that purpose.

Here is the true and cautionary tale of John, who bought a very cheap hand-held GPS over the chandlery counter from a salesman who chortled, 'Look, it is even up-dating here in the shop'. Unless the shop was moving, the reasons for up-date could only be the unit's poor reception and interpretation of data, because of reasons already discussed.

Down at the chart table, the little beast took over forty minutes to acquire a very suspect position because the antenna could not 'see' well enough to lock on to the best available satellites. It was better in the cockpit, but you feel a right twerp holding the device above your head to get a good horizon clear of the coach roof, whilst you steer with your knees and work the sheets and throttle with I know not what — but not for long. The vaunted six-hour battery, died after two.

It cost John £45 to have the case drilled and a 12V adaptor added, then £35 for a mounting bracket, plus £105 for an external antenna kit. He took an afternoon off work (£50) to meet an installation engineer, who paid the marina £10 to park his car and £25 for permission to work (£50) to meet an installation engineer, who paid the marina £10 to park his car and £25 for permission to work on the pontoon. His charge was £33.50 an hour for 2.5 hours. Suddenly, John's £300 toy has cost £650 — and will still not do a serious job well.

The moral of the tale is that technology needs to be seen not just in terms of its own cleverness, but more realistically measured against the yachtsman's actual needs. All innovation must be seaman led rather than electronic engineer led. I can see a limited use for tiny, portable GPS receivers, but not on my boat and certainly not as the principal navigation system of any cruising yacht.

The same questioning judgement must also be used in our acceptance or rejection of Differential GPS (DGPS). It is very clever to be able to put a computer/radio on a very precisely measured spot and to have it broadcast positional corrections to bring GPS back to minute precision. It also seems totally stupid that we should be asked to do it. The American taxpayer ought not to be amused that, having paid an enormous sum to put GPS in place, he pays more to have the purposely induced Selective Availability errors fed into the system, then pays once more to install and maintain a chain of DGPS stations to take the errors out again. Additionally, it costs him more of his income to buy a receiver capable of handling DGPS.

We should also question whether accuracies of ten metres are of any real value to a cruising yachtsman and certainly whether we should pay extra to get them. I can see that a DGPS station guiding me in through the thirty-metre entrance to my own harbour in dense fog might be useful. That, however, connotes a very local, shore-based DGPS station, but how much would that cost and how often are we forced to enter harbour in totally zero visibility? Would the system be worth the extra expense?

We must also think historically. How many lives have been lost, or how much damage caused purely because of yachts/vessels entering harbour in fog? More accidents are due to collision, but there are better ways of avoiding collision than having a master station working on DGPS information. If you have radar to avoid collisions, you also have an excellent tool for feeling your way into port.

We must also call into question the precise accuracy of many charts – both electronic and paper and this especially applies to such things as harbour chartlets which have been drawn by extrapolation and expansion from bigger, smaller scale, charts. What is the point of having a GPS posfix to three digits (two metres but generally reckoned to be fifteen metres in practice) telling you that you are at 50:43.106N and 02:56.913W unless that position coincides exactly with a spot on the chart? Until all charts are drawn to the same datum and until all sub-charts have been physically verified, such pretended precision is a fiction – and that can make life dangerous.

There are a number of practical navigational experiences which well illustrate this argument.

One of the most obvious is to amuse yourself on a coastal trip by taking the lat/long of buoys you will pass from the paper chart and entering them as a waypoint. En route, note how close you are to the buoy when the 'Waypoint Passed' alarm sounds. Then try the same thing on the way home and observe any difference. They are certain to be there, but what is incorrect. Is the GPS giving a wrong position? Is the chart wrong? Has the buoy drifted? Are you sure of your transcription of the co-ordinates? To what datum is the chart drawn? WGS84? OS34? Is your GPS actually set to that datum? Would ten-metre accuracy be of any use in this situation, even if you could interpret it?

Yes; but only if you took the lat/long of the buoy, when you were right alongside it on the outward journey and used DGPS to find it again on the way home. But this is not much use to you if you are entering a strange harbour on instruments and chart.

Our own chart plotter and GPS equipment is amongst the best which money can currently buy, but we are still only as good as the satellite system and the accessories on sale to interpret it will allow. We have a long catalogue of instances when we have entered a harbour by 'eye-balling' our way in, but subsequent examination of our plotter recorded track shows the boat cutting the corner and passing fifty metres across the rocks of a headland. When we switch back from chartlet to chart, the track passes neatly in through the buoyed channel.

To add to the confusion, there are occasions when the passage chart and the large scale harbour chartlet exactly coincide, so you do not really know what to trust, but the discrepancy does give rise to some amusing on-board folklore.

When we lie alongside the wall in our own harbour, Pakman (the name given to the flashing cruciform cursor showing ship's GPS position) sometimes ambles fifty metres towards the harbour office and at other times swans around in the Sailing Club bar some thirty metres south of us. Occasionally, he walks on water in the harbour. This is normal and expected S/A induced aberration.

On the other hand, we spent seven days at anchor in the Mallorcan harbour of Porto Cristo. It appeared that Pakman was fed-up with being at sea, so he skulked off to a building site at least 400 metres away and wandered around it for the whole week. The probable reason is that the plotter's chartlet of Porto Cristo harbour was drawn to a very rough and ready datum point and, therefore, was cartographically in the wrong place. Pakman was located where he should have been on the real Earth, but the chartlet had apparently been slid beneath him.

One gets fed-up with asking whose datum has been used for chart compilation. It is very confusing when you do not really know whose charts to trust, because GPS is better than all of them. This position will get better as all charts are redrawn to the American WGS84 – but this will take time. So, for the moment, we need to live with and to take into account the twin sources of error. Selective Availability and chart aberration.

Luckily, the situation is not quite as black as I have

painted it. There are many excellent, very accurately drawn charts and if you have been to an area once and the chart was good, then it will be good when you return as long as you are aware of S/A effects.

It bears repeating that whereas Decca and other terrestrial systems are often good, their circle of uncertainty can open out to 1.5 miles in the area between Jersey and St Malo and the signal can vanish altogether in certain climatic condition. This just does not happen with GPS. You always know that you are somewhere inside that much publicised 200 metres diameter circle. But is it not great to be able to cross The Atlantic (or The Sahara) and to know where you are to 200 metres no matter what the season of the year, or the time of day?

In closer tolerance navigation, you need to recognise that navigation in its present form is an art, with all the interpretations and tolerances this connotes, rather than a millimetric precise science.

In September 1994, we returned from the Mediterranean, via the Canal du Midi and a 500 mile haul back from Bordeaux to Southern England. Part of this voyage was along the reciprocal of the route partly described in Chapter 8. An account of this adventure appeared in *Practical Boat Owner* the following Spring and has enough tutorial material to make part of this article be worth repeating here.

Those Luddites who slag-off modern electronics as the killer of traditional navigation skills, have it just as wrong as the suicide squad who interface GPS with an autopilot and read comics whilst the boat drives itself. Currently, a combination of ancient and modern ideologies makes navigation safer, faster and more efficient than it has ever been: a cocktail of art, science and experience.

It is at night and in bad weather that you most appreciate the strengths and the weaknesses of both manual and electronic navigation and can even use some of their limitations advantageously. Boat pilotage on instruments is as much a skill to be learned as is chart and pencil skippering. To be safe and sure, you let all the systems and methods (both ancient and modern) check and balance each other.

This need was sharply highlighted during our September return from re-stepping the masts at Pauillac (sur Gironde) and clawing the 500 miles up to Lyme Regis. The weather was at its most mischievous in sending a series of rapidly moving fronts across South Portland and North Biscay. They created a jerky rhythm of short open windows and closed windy doors of gusts and poor visibility. We have travelled this route several times and normally plan to pass all the difficult bits in daylight and with a favourable tide.

This year, the wind and waves decreed otherwise. If we wanted to avoid spending Christmas in France, we had to travel each leg as and when we could.

Abemama is a solid, ketch-rigged 28ft 6in Colvic Watson motor sailer packing a BMC 50 hp diesel – not fast, but very safe. There are only two of us aboard, but we have a robust Cetrek autopilot to take the strain and she is equipped with a Raytheon R20X radar, Phillips MKVI GPS and Cetrek Chartnav plotter. Even though we have plenty of gear, all our passage planning is done on full-size paper charts, with routes, courses, waypoints, co-ordinates and tide vectors both drawn and written in. We also list them in the log. If there is a distance and direction discrepancy between manual and machine, it is generally that I have tapped a wrong key at the data input stage. Thereafter the two systems check each other and we try to use what is best in both.

. . . By 1500 next day, the wind was not obeying the predictions and was both freshening and coming tighter on the nose. The BBC forecast, reinforced by the French VHF outlook, made it obvious that we were not going to make Camaret in one 265-mile hop and that wherever we went we were in for another blow. The best bolt hole was Belle Ile, thirty-five miles to the North.

Once the decision to divert was made, the instruments again came into full play. A flip of the roller ball and a single button push on the Chartnav immediately gave course and distance to Les Galeres, marking the Eastern corner of the island. The plotter's info box also put up its lat/long, gave us the buoy's description and drew an electronic line to it. This was simple to transfer to the APVI which immediately gave an ETA of 2330.

On a rolling boat, when you have been up all night, this means of doing it quickly and electronically was faster and indeed safer than any other way, although I did transfer and check the data on the paper chart when we had settled everything down. Check and balance.

. . . After a day' huge gusts, the met. men promised us at least twenty-four hours of North-Easterly then going SW, with gales again later. Against this prognosis we set off roughly NW on the ninety-five miles around the Pointe de Penmarch to the Raz de Sein and up to Camaret. The promise did not materalise, so we spent a day with main and mizzen sheeted hard, whilst we motor-sailed into a short chop atop a residual swell.

We knew that we should be taking on the Raz in the dark, but the slow progress also made us an hour late on the tide. Our previous experience of the notorious race had always been at slack low water and light wind, but we had heard all the tales of strong streams running in peculiar directions as the flood picks up pace. By this time (0130) the wind had backed North-Easterly and freshened over the tide.

Getting around the actual corner in the dark was not a problem. Both La Vieille and La Plate are distinctively lit and showed well on the radar. For a couple of miles beyond it was uncomfortable, but the Colvic Watson is an exceptionally robust sea boat, so there was no danger in that respect. It was just slow.

The problem was a bows-on dead North and a boat at one time tracking ENE towards the rocky shore North of La Pointe du Raz. In the total disorientating blackness, we could not see the cliffs and the shallows do not show on radar, there was no way of getting a visual fix. Very worrying. But again, the instruments did their job. The

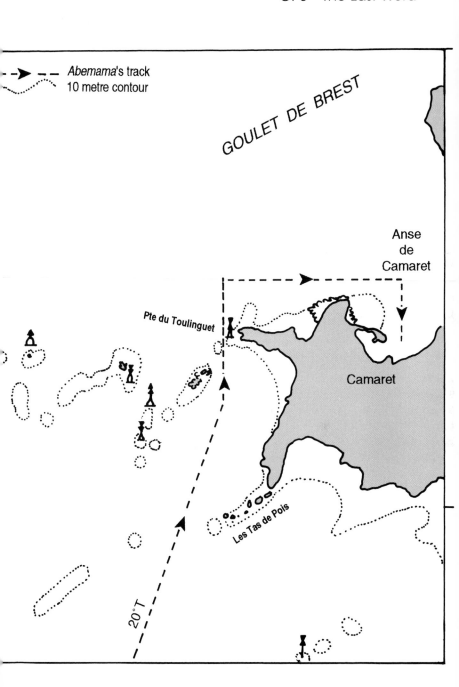

AP Mk VI was giving us good info on the track over the ground and this was also showing clearly on the Chartnav screen. There is plenty of deep water to the West and our fifty horses were well capable of pushing us out into the clear as soon as the problem showed. There was no way we could have been so safe and sure without the electronics and even trying to keep a constant plot on the chart (which I tried) was not really feasible. It was too rough for pencil, ruler and dividers and the positions needed to be penciled in very frequently. It was a good illustration of instrument balance. Decca would probably have been suffering from the rain squalls in addition to its wider circle of imprecision that far South. The GPS and plotter combination were ideal. Without them I would have been disorientated and scared.

This modern, balanced approach to navigation came best into its own on the final leg from the Raz to Camaret. The options are a long northerly haul around Le Trepied and then East along the Rade de Brest, or a slightly shorter route via Chenal du P'tit Leac'h. Both these were very exposed to the North-Easterly wind (now gusting 6–7) plus swell and Leac'h is not a passage which I like because the low rocks are not easy to spot. I would not do it at night.

It was Rita who posed the question 'Do we just bang around down here until daylight and possibly stronger winds, then run to Douarnanez, or can we take on the Passe de Toulinguet in the dark?' This third Raz to Camaret option is a 350 yard-wide passage close in to the headland at the end of a funnel between unlit rocks to the north and the massive Tas de Pois on the right. It promised shelter and calmer water. You steam into a sock and turn left when you get to the heel and can see the holes in the toe. In the narrow Passe itself, there is an unlit west cardinal mark under the lighthouse, where there is deep water and just one isolated, problematic rock awash to the West.

Last time we had come North to Camaret it had been

daylight and calm. Rita eyeballed the boat through the Passe whilst I (just for fun) kept my head down and called out my proposed courses and distances from the waypoints marked on the chart and negotiated with the GPS interfaced to the Chartnav, with the rocks and gaps showing on the radar. Then it had been for fun, now it was for real, but was not scary as long as we used the strengths and weaknesses of the gear available to us.

It bears repeating that the strength is super instruments and the weakness the S/A induced 200m circle of imprecision. It was also totally dark.

From the Raz, the course line to our first waypoint for Toulinguet runs 020°T before turning North. When it first gets into the funnel the very safe clear water is sometimes to port and at others on the right. Current GPS precision is to 2 drms which — as already mentioned — means that you know that you are somewhere inside that 200m circle, but cannot be sure whether you are close to its centre, or out near the circumference. However, for our sort of navigation 200 metres is acceptable for much of the time.

In this instance, the Chartnav was invaluable. On its most rapid up-date setting, it plots a position every 0.5 miles (approx 100m). By ensuring that the track was always at least 200m to the safe side of the plot line, we were able to relax a bit. When the safe water was on the other hand, we simply let boat and track plot drift back across the electronic rhumb line to get into it. This might be a bit belt and braces but it made us feel very safe.

Even though the funnel is composed of individual rocks, from its entrance they look like a continuous wall on the radar screen. As you get closer to having each one abeam, it stands out as an individual. We could count the separate stacks of the Tas de Pois and this gave us a further position fix not only by angle, but by radar calculated distance off.

Further out to part there are a couple of buoys, which also showed on the radar screen. With the Chartnav in navigate mode, a single button push gives distance and heading to the cursor, so we had a confirming check of our position from them, even more backed up with a compass bearing from the KVH Datascope, which has a good night light. With all these systems agreeing with each other, we always knew exactly where we were and where we were heading next even though the night was totally black.

Eventually, we reached our starter waypoint for the turn North and the half-mile jog through the actual 300m wide Passe out into the Goulet de Brest. There was that magic moment when the solid wall of rocks on the radar screen suddenly showed a gap opening up abeam just as Sainsbury (ship's name for the AP MkVI) made his supermarket check-out noise to say that we were at the waypoint and obviously almost in the centre of the 200m circle. The hole grew larger as we turned North and went through it to exit via the toe of our imaginary sock and the west marker also appeared on the screen.

On passage, we fill the GPS memory with the co-ordinates of all the hazards along the way. Then, when we want a bit of back-up info, we call the appropriate one to the screen with a Go-To method and immediately know if we are safe and clear, or if we need to tweak the course. Good, fast modern navigation.

Again the "toys" did the job. Our exit waypoint is well clear of the Passe and clear North of the rocks on the corner of La Pointe de Toulinguet. When we decided to turn East, the Chartnav confirmed that we were well above our rhumb line (normal daytime course) to Camaret and the radar showed us to be 0.5 miles off the coast which we still could not see well enough to orientate.

This was obviously a very satisfying passage to have made, not only because it saved us several hours of very uncomfortable travel and got us to Camaret before the really big wind came, but also because it got everything together. Crew, eyes, chart, pencil, roller-ruler, GPS, plotter, radar and hand compass all working in harmony and checking each other out consistently enough to make any error immediately discernible.

It should also be seen against a number of helpful facts. We have done the Gironde exit, the Raz de Sein and the Passe de Toulinguet a number of times in daylight, so we both have a good mental picture of what they look like. Without this we would probably not have attempted the last bit. We could also totally trust the cartographic accuracy of the C-Map cartridge, which we had used last year. Apart from one fishing boat, there were no other lunatics out near Camaret on such a September night. Anything showing on the radar screen was almost certainly a rock or a buoy. This made interpreting the picture much easier.

In spite of the fact that there is absolutely no way we would have attempted this passage without electronic aids, the Luddites will still say "Ah, but what if you get a fault on a machine, or an electrical failure?" The short answer is that we do not expect this in equipment which has been running well all season and all day. I do not expect to lose the electronic display on my watch and most properly installed and tested marine equipment is as reliable. If something breaks, you stop the boat and try to repair it. If the electric supply goes, we have a rechargeable 10 amp battery pack which would run the instrument bank all day. In extremis, we could plug into the 12 VDC side of the generator. In a real panic, we do just as we have done when a clumsy crew member knocked the sextant off the chart table, or we have seen no sun or stars for days, we revert to all the tricks of good seamanship – including standing away from possible danger. Without them, the expensive toys are dangerous. In conjunction with them, they make life less prone to error, more certain and much safer.'

That has to be the final moral and the final word as GPS stands at the moment and where it will stand for some time to come. We recognise our good fortune in having a truly amazing system of navigation, but must see it in its time and situation. No system yet invented removes the need for good, basic seamanship skills and nobody should be on passage of any sort without satisfactory chart and compass skills. Only with them can you use all electronic aids in general and GPS in particular to their full safe potential.

Chapter 10

GPS Language and Abbreviations

ALARMS

Available on most GPS receivers and can be both visible and audible. A good model will have plenty of scope for changing why the alarm sounds and should cover, battery voltage, antenna fault, autopilot problems, speed too low for battery charge, poor HDOP, no signal up-date and strong wind. There should also be timer alarms (like an alarm clock) and reminders about particular events — eg the weather forecast, approach to a waypoint.

Many people ask why an 'anchor dragging' alarm is not included. The short answer is that Selective Availability makes this impossible.

ALMANAC

A catalogue of satellite information covering such characteristics as satellite time of rise above the horizon, its setting or dipping time, angles of elevation and direction in degrees True from present position. The information is usually good for a month ahead and can be changed by the terrestrial engineers so that the satellite is always sending out very up-to-date information.

ALTITUDE

This means the height of the tip of the receiving antenna above sea level. This is not important in most boats, where there is little difference between sea level and antenna height and is not taken into calculation when the GPS is working in two-dimensional mode. Some cheaper models are unable to come easily out of three-dimensional working and constantly ask for a check on altitude. This especially applies to earlier multiplexing machines, but has now largely been eradicated in properly marinised equipment.

APPARENT WIND ANGLE
The angle of the wind against the side of the vessel as it is modified by the vessel's own (forward) motion and quoted with reference to the vessel's head. An AWA of 00° indicates a wind from right ahead, whereas 180° indicates a wind directly astern. An AWA of 90° could mean that the wind is actually blowing from aft of the beam, but has been 'warped' to a right angle by boat velocity.

APPARENT WIND SPEED
The speed of the wind as modified by the vessel's velocity. For example, if it is blowing onto the stern and the boat is moving forwards, the apparent strength of the wind will be less than its true strength. Similarly, if the wind is forward of the beam of a moving boat, it will read a few knots more than true.

ASCII
The acronymous name derived from the initials of American Standard Code for Information Interchange. It is a computer code agreed by most software designers so that correct alphanumeric data can be passed from machine to machine in an understandable form.

AZIMUTH
The angular distance usually measured from the south point of the horizon by astronomers and from the north point by navigators. In GPS terms it means that angular distance calculated on the circle of the horizon in a clockwise direction from north to the satellite.

BAUD
A unit used to measure the transmission rate of electronic data. One baud is equal to one unit interval per second.

BEARING
The compass direction of any one point from another and is usually (in navigation) quoted as an angle running clockwise from north and expressed in degrees.

BIT
The common term for a binary code digit, which is the smallest segment of information handled by most computer and navigation instrument programs.

CHARACTER STRING
Any continuous series of letters or digits between two spaces.

CHECKSUM
A value symbol transmitted with any message in binary code. It is used at the receiver to check that the message is correctly understood and that it has all been sent. It is a sort of sentence back reader and full-stop combined.

CLICK and BEEP
The usual words for the noise made by the keyboard and the tone verifying that a key has been pressed. Beep is sometimes employed to warn that a wrong key has been operated, or that an incorrect piece of information has been entered.

COARSE/ACQUISITION (C/A) CODE
The set of signals enabling the normal civilian receiver to lock-on to the satellite transmissions and to show a position. If your GPS is used every day, the signals do the job very quickly. On the other hand, our new GPS was tested in Denmark and switched on again in Southern England, where it took seventeen minutes to establish its position. Thereafter, the lock-on time has been less than one minute.

COMPASS DEVIATION
An anomaly in the reading of a magnetic compass caused by factors inherent in the boat. The compass can

be pulled off line by the proximity of metal, a radio loud-speaker, engine electrics or even a carelessly stowed tool box.

COMPASS HEADING
The compass reading before correction for deviation and variation have been taken into account.

CONTROL SEGMENT
The US Department of Defense ground control system for tracking and controlling the satellites. It supplies them with accurate orbital parameters for computation of the ephemerides, which are then sent up to the satellites and down again to the GPS unit.

COURSE
The direction in which a vessel is being steered and is expressed in degrees True or degrees Magnetic in a clockwise direction through 360° from North. In strict navigation language, course applies to the vessel's direction through the water, not the direction intended to be made good, or actually made good, over the ground.

COURSE LINE
Drawn on the chart to display and project the direction to be taken to complete a passage.

COURSE OVER GROUND
Usually shortened to COG and is the actual track of the vessel referenced to the seabed. Such things as a side tide and a wind causing a sailboat to make leeway, often mean that where the vessel is actually being pushed is different from where the head is pointing. GPS follows the tip of the antenna, so it can only report COG.

CPU
Central Processing Unit or the heart of any computer.

CROSS TRACK ERROR
The amount by which a vessel has been pushed, or has drifted away from the rhumb line, or the straight line distance between its start point and its destination. It is measured as the perpendicular distance from the actual position back to the course line.

CURSOR
A flashing symbol showing at which point the computer, or an instrument like a chart plotter is working and where the next piece of information will be inserted, or at which point on the screen, or in the text, the next action will take place.

DATA FIELD
Any defined space, in a computer program or on paper, into which a piece of information of a specified type can be inserted. A data field has a start and a finish point and will usually only accept a certain number of letters, or numbers, or a mixture of both. These parameters are established when the data field is defined. In GPS, all waypoint information is entered into specific data fields — usually one for latitude, one for longitude and others for north and south.

DATUM
The starting, or reference point, on which the co-ordinates used (usually lat/long) to calculate and illustrate position on the earth's surface are based. In most GPS navigators, the basic supplied datum is that used for the American World Geodetic Survey done in 1984 and is referred to as WGS 84. Other datum points are generally included in the software to convert WGS 84 to other reference points decided by cartographers.

DEFAULT
The factory, or basic, setting of the computer. The software assumes that the default setting is acceptable unless the operator gives any other commands.

DILUTION OF PRECISION
A qualitative assessment of the current accuracy of the GPS position and is based on the positions of the separate transmitting satellites and the angles at which their signals cut across each other when transcribed onto a chart. The smaller the DOP, the less the potential error in position precision. Generally speaking, the more spread out the satellites are, the lower the DOP and the more reliable the fix. The most common DOP, and the one used in the navigator, is HDOP — Horizontal Dilution of Precision. HDOP is an indicator of the two-dimensional accuracy in position (latitude and longitude).

EDIT
To modify and amend the data on display for a variety of reasons.

ELEVATION ANGLE
Made by drawing a line from the vessel to the satellite and computing the number of degrees it slants above a horizontal horizon. If the satellite is directly overhead, its elevation is ninety degrees, dropping to zero at the horizon. Satellites which are only about five degrees or less above the horizon are not very reliable as position fixers.

EPHEMERIS (Plural ephemerides)
Used in GPS language to describe a table showing the celestial position and the health of appropriate satellites. It is up-loaded to the satellites every twelve hours and is valid for one day at a time

ETA
Estimated Time of Arrival is a well known expression and is computer calculated based on present speed as indicated by a change of position over a specified time.

FLUXGATE COMPASS
Normally used to give heading information to an autopilot. A coil, or toroid, is excited by a small current and in

turn returns a voltage which varies according to its orientation with the Earth's lines of magnetic force. Its superiority is due to its very fast reaction and absence of swirl. It passes data to a GPS unit via an NMEA interface, which is sometimes a different format from other exchanged information.

TO FORCE HEALTHY
An advanced feature allowing the operator to over-ride the message that a satellite is not suitable for accurate fixes. It should be used with extreme care and only by experienced GPS navigators. Some units also have a program enabling the operator to ignore a strong satellite, but it is difficult to envisage a situation (other than in a test lab) where this could or should be employed for normal GPS use.

GEOGRAPHIC CO-ORDINATES
Now universally accepted as the (chart vertical) parallels of latitude and the (chart horizontal) meridians of longitude on an ellipsoid surface represented as flat by a chart projection. (Usually Mercator) The parallels are also used to measure distances as angular distance, ie raising an imaginary parallel pivoted at the Earth's epicentre by one degree, equates to sixty miles of travel. Traditionally, one minute of latitude has equalled one mile and the fractions of a mile worked in seconds (one sixtieth of a mile). Modern practice works in degrees, minutes and decimal fractions of a minute. In navigational practice, the first has all-but disappeared.

GEOID
The name given to a representation of the Earth's surface with all topographical undulations removed so that all points on the surface approximate mean sea level. It should be seen in tandem with :
GEOIDAL HEIGHT, or variations of the Geoid above and below the mean ellipsoid due to topographical unevenness of the Earth's surface.

GREAT CIRCLE NAVIGATION
Takes advantage of the curvature of the Earth to create the shortest route between points. The disadvantage is that its track may differ from the straight rhumb line that is easily drawn on a Mercator chart. Great Circle navigation is used only for ocean voyages and is very complex at higher latitudes — where it is also most advantageous.

HEADING
The direction in which the vessel is being pointed, expressed as a normal compass bearing. It should not be confused with course, which is an actual, or proposed track. The HEADING is constantly changing as the vessel swings to and fro across the rhumb line because of wind, tide, poor steering or the action of an autopilot.

INTERFACE
The scientific term for 'connected to', but means more than this because it implies a connection which transfers electronic data.

KALMAN FILTER
A software program/device which reduces the acceleration and deceleration effects of boat motion. In effect, it smooths out a display and makes the figures less prone to rapid and confusing change. It works on an agreed range of constants applied to GPS calculations to take account of type of vessel, vehicle or aircraft and its normal characteristics. It is usual to apply constants for:-
A sailing boat
Powerboat, less than 15 knots
Powerboat, 15 to 50 knots
Powerboat more than 50 knots
Trawler type vessel
3-D navigation (recommended for aircraft and cars) or maritime purposes only.

LAYLINE
A word that confuses non-sailing people. It is used to define a line drawn from a destination to a point where a vessel tacking into the wind can make a tack and be able to point at the target. Many GPS units will work out a layline and tell the helmsman when the optimum (theoretical) turning point has been reached. In practice, this is more difficult because of tides, luffing and other characteristics of particular boats and crews.

LCD
Liquid Crystal Display is a screen made of crystals which react to electric current. Most modern watches and many marine instruments have an LCD display comprising hundreds of pixels — or separate lit segments.

LED
Light Emitting Diode is the sort of device which is often used to illuminate electric switches and to make warning lamps.

LOCAL TIME ZONE
The time zone in which the navigator is located and is best illustrated by the common knowledge that France is one hour ahead of UK and, thus, in a different time zone. It has a local offset of one hour and is generally written as minus 01.00, meaning that you must deduct one hour to return to Universal Time Co-ordinated (UTC or UT) which is also GMT and the time system used on board the satellites. The zones comprise twenty-four longitudinal segments around the world, each usually fifteen degrees and one hour wide.

MAGNETIC DEVIATION
A compass error caused by any external factor — metal, radio loudspeaker etc. It should not be confused with magnetic variation, which is the amount by which Magnetic North differs from True North (as shown by the vertical lines on the chart) caused by the annual movement of the Magnetic North Pole.

MENU
A list of functions available in a particular computer or GPS screen display.

MERCATOR
A cartographical map projection used to represent an ellipse as a flat surface. It is seen as a transparent globe with a light at its centre and causing the outlines of countries to be projected onto a vertical cylinder around the globe. It is very functional for navigation because it overcomes the problems of converging meridians, but can produce the distortion that a small country like Greenland can look as large as Africa on the map.

NMEA
The National Marine Electronics Association, which has given its name to an agreed format for the exchange of electronic data.

PARITY BIT
Added to a binary coded message for parity checking purposes and leads to a parity check which is a performed by the software to verify that the binary coded data being transmitted to, is the same as the message being received

P-CODE
The finely tuned (precision) code used in military GPS units to produce the amazing accuracy required for accurate targeting. It is not permitted in civilian equipment.

PSUEDO-RANDOM NUMBER (PRN)
The identification code of a GPS satellite.

RECEIVER
Specifically, the receiver circuit in the navigator which constantly processes the L1 satellite signal — as opposed to the GPS computers which turn this processed data into usable information.

RHUMB LINE
A course, or a planned passage, which is drawn as a straight line on a chart and passes across all meridians at the same angle.

ROOT MEAN SQUARED
A statistical measure of probability, stating that an expected event will happen 68% of the time. In terms of present GPS use, 68 position updates out of 100 will be accurate to within specified system accuracy.

ROUTE
Used in GPS navigation to define a series of linked way-points along which it is planned to travel — in either direction.

S/A
The short form of Selective Availability.

SAILPLAN
A term much like route, or a series of joined routes.

SATELLITE CONSTELLATION
Any group of satellites being tracked by a receiver/processor. Its size is usually either three, four, five, or six satellites.

SELECTIVE AVAILABILITY (S/A)
The system which reduces the accuracy of GPS position information. S/A is controlled by the US Department of Defense and can be switched on and off from the ground control stations. S/A can generally be expected to create a circle of uncertainty measuring 200 metres in diameter.

SIGNAL-TO-NOISE RATIO
A quantitative relationship between the useful and non-useful part of the received satellite signal. A high S/N indicates a good signal strength.

SPEED OVER GROUND
Speed in relation to the seabed — usually abbreviated to SOG.

TIME OFFSET
The number of hours by which the time zone differs from Universal Time Co-ordinated.

VDU
Visual Display Unit is any screen which shows data.

VISIBLE SATELLITE
A satellite whose orbit places it high enough above the horizon to be on a straight line to the navigation unit's antenna at the present time.

WAYPOINT
Any point along a proposed route, including the start and finish. It is also used to describe any other position stored in a GPS navigator's memory, or defined on a chart.

WAYPOINT CLOSURE VELOCITY (WCV)
The speed at which the vessel is getting nearer to the waypoint and is used to describe approach velocity in — say — the case where a sailboat is tacking and thus slanting towards the target.

WAYPOINT PASS CRITERIA
The method by which the navigator tells the operator that a waypoint has been passed, even though the vessel might not have exactly cut through this point.

WORLD GEODETIC SYSTEM (WGS)
(sometimes called World Geodetic Survey)
These are world-wide datums (WGS 72 and WGS 84) used for satellite navigation. The main difference is a small eastward shift. The resulting difference in position will normally be 0.01 minutes longitude, which will not

be noticeable on charts of scale 1:50,000 or smaller. You may thus use the WGS 84 Plus Offset datum with charts marked with a WGS 72 offset. All charts will probably eventually be converted to WGS 84 datum.

NORMALLY USED ABBREVIATIONS

AWA	Apparent Wind Angle
AWS	Apparent Wind Speed
AZ	Azimuth
BFT	Beaufort
BRG	Bearing
COG	Course Over Ground
Datum	Latitude/Longitude reference as stated on chart in use
Dev	Deviation
DHMS	Days, Hours, Minutes and Seconds
dir	Direction
DIST	Distance
EL	Elevation angle above horizon
ETA	Estimated Time of Arrival
Fm	Fathom (60 ft = 1.8288 m)
Ft	Feet (0.3048 m)
Gal	US or Imperial Gallon
GPS	Global Positioning System
HDG	Heading
HDG-C	Heading Compass
HDG-M	Heading Magnetic
HDOP	Horizontal Dilution of Precision
hm	Time in hours: minutes
hms	Time in hours, minutes and seconds
ht	Height
Km	Kilometre
Kn	Knot
Kmh	Kilometres per hour
Log	Water speed log
ltr	Litre
m	Metre
m/s	Metres per second
Mi	Statute Mile (1605 m)
min	Minute
MOB	Man Over Board
Mph	Statute Miles per hour
NAD	North American Datum

Nm	Nautical miles (1852 m)
OSGB	Ordnance Survey of Great Britain
Pos	Position
PRN	Satellite Pseudo Random Noise identification number
SAD	South American Datum
sec	Time in seconds
S/N	Signal to Noise ratio in dBHz
SOG	Speed Over Ground
TTG	Time To Go
TWA	True Wind Angle
TWD	True Wind Direction
TWS	True Wind Speed
UNC	Uncertainty
U	Unhealthy Satellite
UTC	Universal Time Co-ordinated
Var	Magnetic variation
VMG	Velocity Made Good
WCV	Waypoint Closure Velocity
WGS	World Geodetic System
WPT	Waypoint(s)
XTE	Cross Track Error

Index